DEATH BY THOUSAND LIES

MY COVER UP, MY CRASH AND MY RESURRECTION FROM SEXUAL ADDICTION

by Blaine Bartel

Love you guys!

DEDICATION

Lori
They don't know my head is a mess.
They don't know who I really am.
And they don't know what I've been through.
Like you do.
And I was made for you.

Jeremy
Only with you. Never without you.

Dillon
The only thing that transcends your courage is your love.

Brock
I'm proud to be your father, beyond blessed to be your friend.

Ally
The daughter I always hoped for.

Mum
You never let go. The reason I'm still here.

Dad
Your kindness. Wow.

Lord Jesus
For grace that rolled my stone away.

THANK YOU

Each of you helped remove the grave clothes.

Cathy Bartel
Michael and Becca Caney
Ron and Katie Luce
Dr. Ken McGill
Jon and Lisa Purkey
Ed and Gail Gungor
Brent and Janis Sharpe
Gregory and Grace Dickow
Ruth Graham
Ted and Gayle Haggard
Pastor Willie and Deleva George
Scotty and Jamie Gurele
Eddie and Dawna Elguera
Adam and Michelle Palmer
Whitney and Heather George
Kevin Cortez
Roy Evans
Doyle and Lucy Bishop
Chuck and Annette Tate
Gordie and Kathleen Lagore
Scott Wesley
Steve and Tammi Miller
Erik Lawson
Dave and Joan Styles
Dave Lagore
Dr. Ralph Earle
Dr. Ken Wells

ACKNOWLEDGMENTS

Special thanks to the following people who
helped make this book possible.

Tommy Hernandez
For your design expertise and my many changes on the cover.

Adam Palmer
For your help with editing and teaching me a little
more about writing.

Ed Cyzewski
For investing in the manuscript and the proper telling of
my story.

Kickstarter Friends
You made this possible. I can't thank you enough.

My Family
For allowing me to include you in my story.

Dr. Ken Wells
For being my counselor, my mentor and my friend.

CONTENTS

FOREWORD

The book you hold in your hands is a raw story of a man's agonizing struggle with the demons of pornography and lust. If you're not comfortable with a very honest account of Blaine's desperate fight for freedom, put the book down.

His twenty year addiction to sexual vice created a deep emotional contradiction because of his own vibrant Christian faith and international leadership in youth ministry. How could he possibly live in both worlds?

Blaine is honest about it all.

If you have experienced this struggle, been victimized by it or you know someone in it, I would strongly encourage you to read on.

It's raw. It's real. It's graphic.

I know Blaine to be an honest man, broken by his addiction. I know him to be a man of God. Blaine discovered that Jesus never let him go. The Lord has brought him to a beautiful place of cleansing and release.

I hope you will allow these words to give you hope that your addiction can be defeated and find life-long victory over this hellish trap. It won't be easy—he makes that abundantly clear.

But if you are honest with yourself and truthful with those who love you, I believe the words in this book will put you on path for the freedom you've always longed for.

Sincerely,

Ruth Graham
Ruth Graham Ministries

Before the truth can set you free,
you need to recognize
the lies that hold you hostage.

—Rachel Wolchin

PROLOGUE

This is an honest story. A brutal one in it's worst moments.

I am not the hero of my story. Others will fill that role. You will be as disappointed in me as you are in yourself at times. I tell my story with distress and discomfit, but my goal in telling it is uncomplicated.

Whether you are a man or a woman, the lies that you tell yourself and others to hide the shame of your sexual brokenness will eventually lay claim to every scrap of happiness ... every breath of life ... you have left.

We never fully fathom the sheer beauty of resurrection until we come to grips with the absolute disfigurement of death. There is no glory in my past. But somehow there is a prodigal-son-gratitude in the remembering.

Our found-ness is fully treasured when we concede our lost-ness.

Not in a reminiscing way, but in celebration of a death-defying Savior.

At times my language will be offensive to some. Not to insult your virtues. Never gratuitous. And not in any attempt to provide shock value. Why then? At times, that's honestly how the story unfolded and sugar-coating it will diminish it's harsh reality. Other times, releasing my "inner F-bomb" is only way I can be linguistically truthful about my emotions. Hey, when life buries you six feet under, one tends to develop a more descriptive vocabulary for the dirt one is eating.

Though I share my story from a Christian perspective, (because that's all I know) along with occasional texts from the ancient writ, please be assured it is not my goal to convert or preach to you. If you are not a follower of Jesus, I respect and honor wherever you are right now in your spiritual journey. Finding our way in this world can be as nutty as a squirrel's turd. I get that. Just know—one human being to another—I'm for you.

Lastly, some of the names have changed. Because they would not want to be named. And I don't want to be sued.

The prologue is getting too long. Let's go.

Scene One

THE COVER UP

"The monarchy is finished. It was finished a while ago, but they're still making the corpses dance."

—Sue Townsend

Chapter One
YES, REGINA.

I was born in Regina, Saskatchewan. That's in Canada. I know … the city has kind of a weird name. Especially when you tell people you were "born in Regina." And they look back with a smirk and say, "Of course you were."

I came out of the womb with a hockey stick and my Dad tossed me a puck. I grew up with a passion for sports. All of them. Hockey, football, lacrosse, baseball, tennis, judo, freestyle skiing, wrestling, gymnastics, volleyball, golf, racquetball … heck, I would have played finger-jousting if they had offered it. Wait … I did play finger-jousting.

I loved to compete. It was my oxygen.

By the time I was 16 years old, I had won provincial championships in Judo and Freestyle Skiing. I had this God-given ability to beat people up and then entertain them with a double front flip 30 feet in the air on skis.

I hated second place. Second place trophies wouldn't even make the mantle. Jerry Seinfeld nailed it in his comedy special in his bit about The Olympics, "When you win silver it's like, 'Congratulations, you almost won. Of all the losers—you came in first of that group. You're the number one loser. No one lost ahead of you!'"

I must have got some of my competitive fire from my Dad. He grew up in Govan, Saskatchewan and quit school in ninth grade. But he was determined to make something of himself. The best decision he ever made was marrying my Mum. She was a catch of a beautiful woman and brought out the best in Dad. Together they were taking on the world, ninth grade education and all.

And they began to win.

By the time I was in my teens, Dad owned several restaurants, we had a super-rad house with a pool (hockey rink in winter) and being the oldest of the three kids, I was already being groomed to help Dad run his businesses. At twelve years old, I began as a dishwasher and worked my way up to one of the lead cooks by the time I was fifteen. When my friends were out playing and partying on weekends, I was cashing paychecks.

I found out cash is king. On my sixteenth birthday, I had saved enough money to buy a 1970 Dodge Duster. 0 to 60 in about an hour. Not the fastest car in the world, but hey … I was the first kid in my grade to drive his own car. Instant girlfriend magnet. My friends called me "Big B" and I thrived on the popularity.

Mum and Dad were proud of me. And why not? Hard working kid. Decent grades. Great athlete.

And unhappy as hell.

With no idea why.

Chapter Two
SOMEONE SAVED MY LIFE TONIGHT

I don't remember much about McKillop United Church in Lethbridge, Alberta, Canada. Preserved in my mind are a handful of vague memories of my time there.

My Sunday school teacher was pretty.
I stole a nickel out of the offering once.

What I remember most was sitting in the mind-numbing services with my family, forgetting the hardness of the pews by looking at the sunlight filtering through the floor-to-ceiling stained glass windows to create a transcendent work of art. Each piece of glass became a conduit of dazzling color that, on a bright Sunday morning, would fill the sanctuary with a sort of divine brilliance. Little did I know these windows would later become some sort of weird metaphor for my life.

I had no idea as a ten-year-old boy that the church world would become my life. That the church would save me and, in a strange way, that I would eventually allow it to slay me.

Five years later, my fifteen-year old punk self began to find holes in my parents' religion. Too many of them. What I saw in church just didn't match with the real world. I guess I just started thinking for myself and began to ask the hard questions about life, love and sexuality.

One day, while working at one of the restaurants my father owned, something happened that shook me to the core.

I had this boss named Jack. Super cool guy. I had always looked up to Jack. He was the kind of boss that was fun to be around. When the shift ended on one unforgettable Friday night, Jack asked if I wanted to spend the night with him and his girlfriend and drink some beer together. I was like, "Really? Heck yea!" After a couple beers and some joking around at the kitchen table, I retreated to the spare bedroom in the early morning hours.

Sometime after falling asleep, I felt another body slip into bed with me and start to move their hands from my shoulders slowly down my back. Still slightly dazed and half asleep, I muttered, "Who is that … what's going on?" It was Jack.

He quietly assured me, "It's alright Blaine … just relax." Relax? What the hell.

As his hand moved around my waist, he began to touch my genitals. All I can remember is being somewhere between bewildered and WTF?? What should I do? This is my boss.

My Dad has hired him. He was a good guy. And he had a girlfriend. What is going on here?? Wait a minute. Is he touching my stuff? Holy shit!!!

My confused fifteen-year old self finally roused to consciousness and jerked out of the bed. I felt shame and embarrassment. I finally just uttered, "Hey Jack, I need you to stop doing that ok?" As if I had to ask his permission not to be molested. He stood up and quickly moved towards the door, remarking, "Hey Blaine, no problem. Let's just keep this between you and I, ok?" "Yea, for sure," I responded absolutely mortified at what had just happened.

And I would not tell a soul about that night for thirty-five years. But not a week passed in thirty-five years without the shame of that evening finding it's way into my messed up mind.

Why did he pick me? Was I broken in some way? The first sexual advance in my life had just come from a man who was twice my age and trust me … it screwed with my head.

Following that episode, I began to feel myself slowly slipping into a really deep depression. All I wanted to do was sit on the orange shag carpet in my bedroom and spin an Elton John record over and over again: *Someone Saved My Life Tonight*. I remember looking out my bedroom window, wondering why living could feel this horrible.

By now, my Mum had been overcome by severe depression as well. I thought to myself, Did feeling-like-shit just run in our family? She would not come out of her bedroom for days on end. When she did emerge, I just remember seeing so much sadness on her face. So much sadness. My father was working long days and most weekends trying to get our family ahead in life. I probably saw my Dad more at work than I did at home.

I never resented him for it. I thought it was normal. Work your ass off. Get ahead. Win at all costs.

And then, one day while riding down the road and looking out the window at the passing scenery, I had a spiritual epiphany:

There is no way God exists.

How could he? Not in this screwed up world. Church was a sham. Take your weak-assed conscience to some holy building with a cross and listen to a feel-good sermon to get your guilty mind through another week.

I became an atheist, though I probably couldn't have even spelled the word. I'm sure Jesus was a great guy, but so was Jack and look how that turned out. The God-hippie with sandals who lived shortly after the dinosaurs was no different than Santa Clause. Another story passed down by parents to kids until the kids wised up and realized there is no North Pole—and there is no Heaven.

So that was that. Until one year later. Without warning, my notion of a world without God would be radically turned on it's head.

I got saved.

Not Baptist saved. Not Methodist saved. Born-again, tear-steaming, snot-shooting Pentecostal saved. (not saying Methodists and Baptists aren't saved) The thing I recall most—besides the sweaty weight of numerous hands on my head and the organist wailing on "Amazing Grace"—was the pure love of Christ that seemed to course through my entire soul.

I'm not making this up. For the first time in my life, I was pretty damn sure God loved me. It was like I felt all the depression, pain, and disillusionment being washed away forever.

But forever is a long time.

From that moment on, I lived my life believing that Jesus Christ was the hope of every person. And for reasons beyond my comprehension, I eventually found myself catapulted into prominence as a young torchbearer in the evangelical church world.

Jesus had changed me. And I was about to change the world. My Mum was thrilled. My Dad not so much.

Chapter Three
SOMETHING TO PROVE

While Jesus had changed my heart, he hadn't done a dang thing for my grades.

I completely lost interest in school by twelfth grade. I skipped more than half of my classes and saw my grade average plummet to 26% by second semester. Yes … that means I was getting 74% of all my answers wrong. How is that even possible? People can guess better than that.

I was completely wrapped up in freestyle skiing. All I wanted to do at the time was load up my skis and go to the mountains every day, in hopes of becoming a national champion. And then this happened. I came home and announced to my Mum and Dad that I had quit school. To become a champion. National champion. They were thrilled. (insert sarcasm emoji here) And proceeded to explain to me that I would now need to get a job to support myself, since I had given up on the idea of being educated. Of course they said it in the most loving way.

So I found work at a steel factory. I had a love-hate relationship with my new job. I loved leaving every day and I hated showing up. It was loud, dirty and the hardest work I'd ever done. I felt like Jonah in the belly of the steel whale. So I made new plans. I quit my job. I quit skiing. I went to Southern California. I spent the next year at Youth With a Mission and took the Jesus life to a whole new level.

In YWAM, the code word was "radical." How committed to Jesus are you? Are you fasting, praying, preaching and reaching? Add to that my introduction to Keith Green, a revolutionary Christian music troubadour whose debut album, *No Compromise* called to task every lukewarm, milquetoast, backslidden, half-hearted believer to a militant faith in Jesus. And I bought in hook, line, sinker, fishing boots, boat and ocean.

When I returned home one year later, I was determined to finally secure God's approval of my life. The devil be damned. I was preaching on the streets of downtown Calgary and cornering unsuspecting sinners in the Slurpee section at 7-11's. The gospel had to be preached. People were going to hell and their blood was on my hands if I didn't have the courage to tell them about Jesus. I called together a committed group of Christian friends from church and started a ministry team. Within months, I had a local access television show, crusades at community centers and a ministry newsletter.

And then there was the night in our basement jacuzzi. By this time, both my Mum and Dad had come to my new Pentecostal church and both walked the well-worn path to the altar and gave it all to Jesus. Something very real happened in their lives. Mum's depression lifted as the Lord began to fill her with a joy and purpose that would remain in her life to this very day. And Dad took his foot off the accelerator at work and began to spend more time with our family, as well as serving as a deacon in our church. My sister Luanne had become a happy-clappy Jesus person too, while my brother Jason was not buying into the whole Christian thing just yet. His time would come.

Dad and I had begun smacking the racquetball around every week and we would often come back to the house and soak our tired bodies in the jacuzzi. We always had good conversations.

Dad was—and to this day is—the kindest and most thoughtful man I know. But on this night with jacuzzi jets roaring, he blew a gasket. I announced my plans to go into full-time Jesus work, which meant I would not be saddling up any longer in the family business.

Voices were raised.
Water splashed.
And I bolted.

All I remember is throwing on my clothes and running out of the house to take a long walk around Lake Bonavista, which was a mile from our house. What was wrong with my father? Where was his commitment level to Christ, anyways? I remembered the words of Jesus, "Everyone who has left houses or brothers or sisters or father or mother or wife or children or fields for my sake will receive a hundred times as much and will inherit eternal life." (Matthew 19:29) My earthly father may not be happy about this, but all of heaven was applauding.

And although I never voiced this, on some level deep inside my soul, I wanted to prove to my Dad that I could be a success without him. Everyone knows the stereotypes for people in ministry. They are poor. Probably couldn't make it anywhere else. Just happy to live an obscure and humble existence. Well not this cat. I had every plan to shatter the glass ceiling.

One month later I would meet a man who would put the sledge hammer in my hands. And the ceiling would come down.

Chapter Four
COMING TO AMERICA

Waiting at the customs exit at Calgary's International Airport, I had no idea what was about to happen. I was getting ready to meet the man who would basically give me a blank check to finally change the world. He didn't know it. I didn't know it. I'm going to guess God knew and I wonder what He thought about it at the time.

As Willie George walked out the custom doors, I recognized him right away from the picture on the brochure I was holding in my hands. Willie had been invited by our church to conduct a children's crusade and speak to a large group of kids workers over the weekend. I was asked by our church Sunday School super-intendent to be his helper for the weekend. So my job was to get him around in my sweet '79 brown Chevy van, help set up his puppet stage and resource table, take him to eat … you know … be Alfred for Batman for a couple days.

By the time the weekend ended, I was in awe of this man. He talked my language. Willie was a charismatic leader with a co-lossal vision to change the world. He was extremely creative and resourceful, but more than all of that, he kind of took to me. He had a fatherly spirit about him, even though he was only nine years older than I was. As I took him back to the airport Sunday after church, he invited me to join his ministry team, which was headquartered in Tulsa, Oklahoma.

Wow. Let's rewind a bit.

Three months earlier, I married Cathy Hunt. We grew up in high school together and she was literally the girl of my dreams. About six months before Cathy and I began dating, I had a dream that I married her. "Could this be a sign from God," I wondered? Well, I really hoped it was because I would have done anything to date her in high school. But I never had a chance. She went out with the middle linebacker on the football team and he was a stud. But something had happened in Cathy's life following high school. She had this deep desire to serve Jesus in ministry and had put her dating life on the shelf.

She had become of part of my band of merry little Jesus proclaimers and it wasn't long before I proposed to her. We married a few months later and we began talking about going to Bible School in Tulsa, Oklahoma. We were ready to go "all in" for Jesus.

So when the invitation came from Willie George to serve on his team in Tulsa … jackpot!! And I do mean jackpot. Within a few short years, our ministry machine rolled all sevens and we were big time in the national world of youth ministry.

Based on what happened next, I imagine the devil laughed with glee.

Chapter Five

FIRE BY NITE FAME

Growing up, a kid wants to be a lot of things. Early on, I was going to be a Mountie. You know, like Dudley Do-Right from *The Rocky and Bullwinkle Show*? OK, never mind. But as I grew older, I was determined to find a way to make it as an actor in Hollywood. Looking back, I kind of grew up craving the spotlight. I don't know if it was fame I was after or if I just despised the thought of being ignored in this world. But I always had this ambition to be the quarter in a pocket full of pennies.

Suddenly with my attention turned to Jesus and taking the gospel to the world, I think these aspirations simply got redirected. I wanted to make Jesus famous, but also knew in doing so, I would be famous too, right? So when we moved to Tulsa, our new ministry mentor, Willie George, began producing *The Gospel Bill Show*, a television program for children, which would quickly catch on across the nation. The show was basically Jesus on a horse. With a cowboy hat. And a gun with no bullets.

Each show was set in the old west and Willie played Gospel Bill, the born again, spirit-baptized Sheriff of Dry Gulch. Actually the program was done pretty well, considering the limited budget. Each show had a Christian message that resonated with children and parents everywhere. It was also a chance for me to test my acting chops. Casting for the show was pretty simple. The producer would walk around the ministry offices and pick people to play parts in the drama. So we had accountants playing horse thieves and worship leaders playing deputies.

My favorite two acting parts were "Johnny Bob McElroy" and "Lightning Lou Haynes." Johnny Bob was somewhat of a regular character who was known as the prankster-loving teenager of Dry Gulch. And Lighting Lou was the lead bad guy in the episode, "When Evil Comes." I led a gang that was out to take Gospel Bill down and sack his town of Dry Gulch. In the end, Gospel Bill won. Because he always won. Because he wrote the scripts.

In the next few years, my heart would be turned toward reaching teenagers. I began doing "Rock Music Exposed" crusades, decrying the evils of modern rock and "backward masking" (finding hidden Satanic messages by playing the music backwards—I know, I know.) People began to tell me I had a certain gift to reach young people. As Willie and I talked about my future, we had this idea to use the same TV equipment they were using to shoot The Gospel Bill Show to produce a top notch program that would impact teenagers.

We launched *Fire by Nite*. (God led his people in the old testament with a cloud by day and fire by night - we misspelled night because … purposely misspelling stuff is cool. Right?) Somehow, we were able to talk three hundred churches into purchasing a video copy for $25 bucks each. We had a pretty original concept in mind:

Start with *Saturday Night Live*.
Mix in Jesus.

I remember hearing from a youth pastor a couple years later who thought we had stolen his idea to do a Christian version of *Saturday Night Live*. I just laughed. Yea, you and a thousand other youth pastors had the idea. We just happened to be the first ones to give it a shot.

Our very first show featured yours truly, lamely attempting a David Letterman style opening monologue, followed by a few comedy skits, a family sit-com, a song and interview with a Christian music artist named Carman and a gospel message at the end. It wasn't amazing, but it didn't suck either. Which was pretty good for Christian television at the time.

Five years later, we were mailing out five thousand videos a month and it was being broadcast nationally on nearly all the Christian networks and stations. The Armed Forces Network even carried it on their broadcast schedule internationally. Millions of people were now exposed to our ministry as *Fire by Nite* swept through the nation like wildfire.

And my life blew up.

Chapter Six

MY DRUG OF CHOICE

My telephone was ringing more than a Catholic church bell at Easter.

I was cashing in my *Fire by Nite* notoriety with all kinds of speaking engagements in the US, Canada and around the world. My challenging message and modern methods of presenting the gospel were connecting with young audiences everywhere. And I was being invited into relationships with the who's who of Christendom.

Over the next few years, I would speak in more than twenty countries and every state in the Union, except Alaska. (What's wrong with you Alaska people?) I was a regular keynote at Christian student conferences and festivals, including Creation Festival, where I spoke to 60,000 young people. Basically it was Woodstock baptized in the Holy Water. I was also invited to speak to 100,000 young people on the steps of the Capital in Washington, DC. Add to that numerous TV and radio appearances along with featured articles in national publications … this was all pretty heady stuff for a twenty-eight year old guy.

I had become a celebrity, and perhaps the worst kind of celebrity: a Christian one.

The truth is, even at the height of my so-called success, I never really thought twice about the strange mix of Christianity and celebrity. I just kind of embraced it. Being somewhat of a Christian idol grew on me and afforded me all kinds of opportunities and perks. Nearly everywhere I would go, someone would recognize me and usually ask for an autograph. It was weird channel surfing on Friday night and seeing your own face pop up on the television, but I liked it.

It was around this time that I met Ron Luce. Ron worked at a local Tulsa radio station and was a graduate of Oral Roberts University. We fueled each other's passion to reach teenagers, and we became closer than brothers. He was smitten with the idea of taking young people on mission trips around the world. So I asked Ron to do a segment on *Fire by Nite* called "What's Hot!" Each episode Ron would update our young audience on music and entertainment culture. Then, at the end of his short segment, he would invite them to join him on one of his summer missions trips.

And Teen Mania was birthed. The first summer, we helped Ron recruit 300 students to share the gospel in Guatemala. We took our TV crew and filmed it all, telling the story on *Fire by Nite* when we returned. Over the next five years, Teen Mania snowballed. It wasn't long before thousands of students were becoming Teen Maniacs every summer. Eventually Ron's ministry and outreach would become the biggest thing going in American student ministry. His newly minted "Acquire the Fire" (ATF) conference would mushroom in cities across North America, reaching more than three million students in its historic run.

Ron recruited me as a regular speaker at ATF. We loved each other like brothers and trusted each other. In the end, Teen Mania would crumble under the financial weight of so many outreaches and Ron's exhausting challenge of trying to keep up with it all. But he and his wonderful wife Katie made history. Only heaven knows all the lives they impacted. I know they did mine.

Ron knew everything about me. Except for one secret. Twenty-four years after our first meeting, he would discover that secret in the board room of Teen Mania's executive offices. It was in that moment that I fully realized the kind of friend Ron really was.

I'm going to be honest with you. There was money to be made in celebrity ministry. By now my salary was around six figures, plus I was collecting honorariums every weekend from churches and event organizers. And then there were all the product sales we would collect at our events. And the group of ministers I ran with at the time, scripturally associated wealth with the blessing of God. So an abundance of money equaled God's approval on some level.

And I thought back to my father. I had proved myself right In just a few short years I planted my victory flag on top of the world for all to see. I wasn't sure why I had this feeling inside that I needed to compare and compete with him. The fact was, he gave me no reason to do so. He and Mum had not only accepted my decision to pursue the ministry, but had become my biggest fans. But achievement had become my drug of choice. It fueled me.

Each new opportunity, increase or advancement was like a needle in my veins. I was slowly falling in love with the accolades and the applause.

And slowly falling out of love with Jesus. And my wife.

Chapter Seven
FAMILY LAST

My wife, Cathy, and I played brother and sister characters in our sit-com on *Fire by Nite*. She was Connie and I was Doug. Patterned after *Family Ties*. I was the "Christian" Michael J. Fox (Alex Keaton) and Cathy was Justine Bateman (Mallory). Except our dramatic ditty was called "Family First." This part of FBN was without question the most popular segment of the show. We actually had some pretty good comic actors, including John and Vicci Jo Witty (our parents on the show) and Chris Theis (Doug's nerdy best friend).

While the sit-com demonstrated the ideals of God and family, I was doing anything but putting my own family first.

My family had become last.

I was allowing my every waking hour to be filled with my steady climb to the peak of ministry success. Monday through Thursday each week was filled with script writing, shooting the program and spending late nights with our extraordinary director, Steve Yake, editing the program. By "editing" I mean having coffee while he edited—and throwing in my occasional opinion on how a segment should piece together. Steve and I became the best of friends. His father was the director of Teen Challenge in Pennsylvania and Steve had a deep love for the ministry we were doing. He would eventually go on to become the "go to" guy for the burgeoning Christian music video scene.

Artists like Michael W. Smith, Carman and Petra would come and do our show—and Steve would shoot a music video for them while they were in Tulsa. It was a win-win for all. We had all the top Christian artists begging to be on our show. And a win for me. I was asked to host music award events and speak on con- cert tours with bands like The Newsboys.

After each grueling week of production with FBN, I would take off Friday to some city in North America to speak on the week- end, which routinely included a Friday night youth rally, a Sat- urday student conference, and a Sunday church service. I would fly out Sunday afternoon landing at Tulsa International late that evening exhausted. And the madness would start all over again Monday morning.

It was during the *Fire by Nite* years that Cathy and I would be blessed with three extraordinary boys: Jeremy, Dillon and Brock. We loved our boys and they were all model kids growing up. We were always being complimented on their behavior and engaging personalities. Jeremy was a creative soul who grew up making video skits on our camcorder, with his brothers serving as his actors. Dillon had a tender grace about him and loved music and dance … and talking on the phone to his innumerable company of friends. Brock was the athlete of the trio and was always the pop-ular kid in his school and classes. But these three were more than brothers. They were best friends—and still are today.

As busy as I was, I really did try to be a good father. I would go to their sports events or music performances when I was home. We were a very affectionate family—kisses on cheeks and hugs coming and going—and "I love you" was a daily part of our vo- cabulary. Whenever I could, I took one of my boys on a speaking trip with me. On one occasion, Jeremy, who is my oldest, asked if he could fly out with me to Los Angeles. He wanted to see one of the big movie studios. He was about 14 at the time and had a dream of being a Hollywood filmmaker. I made a few calls and was able to secure a private tour of Steven Spielberg's Dreamworks Studios.

That weekend with Jeremy (a.k.a. "Bub") was a magical father and son time. Jeremy was wide-eyed to say the least, as we observed these world-class artists story-boarding and editing the next great movies about to hit the theaters. When we got back to the hotel, I remember inviting Bub to join me on our knees at the bed to pray together over his future. As we drove down Hollywood Boulevard later that evening, I reminded him … that if he would just put God first in all of his plans, all of his dreams of being a great filmmaker could be a reality.

Looking back on that conversation today, I have mixed feelings. I feel as though I was constantly putting success as a carrot on the end of the *obey God stick* with my boys. "If you just obey God and stay out of sin, He will give you your dreams," seemed to be my refrain. A spiritual quid pro quo. If I had a do-over, I think I would just live a more passionate life for Jesus and a less passion- ate chasing of success. While I believe serving Jesus can result in great blessing in our life, it also results in martyrdom in many places in our world.

Perhaps we should encourage our children to follow Jesus simply because he loves them and he is good.

Jeremy has since gone on to become one of the most respected writers and video/film directors in the Southwest. He is working out his own spiritual path, and I am proud of him.

In spite of my attempts to be the husband and father I wanted to be … I needed to be … my achievement and notoriety-seeking soul kept me from being my best. And it wasn't long until burnout and exhaustion would place demands on my soul that I was completely unprepared for.

It began on a Saturday night. In a hotel room somewhere in America. With a little red button.

Chapter Eight
LITTLE RED BUTTON

I gave another message at another conference in another city and went back to another hotel room. I honestly don't remember the hotel, nor the city I was in, nor the theme of the conference, nor the title or content of the message I gave. When you're as busy as I was at the time, these things all blend together.

I was drained.
My mind was drained.
My body was drained.
My spirit was drained.

I was always pushing the limits. I can't even count the number of times I've run out of gas in my car. I could always go a couple more miles before filling up, only to discover optimism doesn't fuel an automobile engine.

Now the fuel gauge of my life was below "E." I refused to pay attention to the unhealthy signs. I was running on fumes, and I was a perfect target.

I had a ritual I would go through after I spoke—I would head back to the hotel and wind down by sitting on the edge of the bed, taking the remote control in hand, and flipping through the channels.

It was less about finding something to watch and more about shutting down my public persona and taking in the hypnotic calm that came from that rhythmic click … click … click …

Just about every time I would cycle through the channels until I landed on ESPN to catch up on the scores and news from that day's sporting events.

But not tonight. I was so exhausted from my schedule that I had almost no spiritual fight left in me, no troops to muster in case of temptation. Instead, it was this:

Click … sports.
Click … game show.
Click … news.
Click … pay-per-view porn options.

Pause.

Click … infomercial.
Click … C-SPAN
Click … infomercial.
Click … pay-per-view porn options.

Pause.

Click … news.
Pause.
Click … pay-per-view porn options.
Pause.

Get up from my bed. Walk over to the box. On top of the television. With the little red button. That damnable red button.

Press.

There they were, exploding onto the screen:

Beautiful women. Welcome to more than twenty years of an ever-spiraling addiction.

Nothing was left to the imagination. They asked for nothing in return.

They were there for me. I was hooked.

I watched. Within minutes, I masturbated, then quickly turned the damned thing off. This was way, way too easy. My flesh grinned salaciously. Blaine, what took you so long? My spirit grieved repentantly. God, what have I done? A fight broke out between the two. The images swirled through my mind, creating what felt like an insatiable craving, while my spirit cried out to God for mercy and forgiveness to be saved from hell.

No, seriously: I literally thought I was going to hell.

I was supposed to be better than the rest. I was a man of God, a shepherd called to lead the flock—how had I allowed myself to become as dirty as a truck stop toilet? How could I ever hold my head up again? How could I ever stand before a crowd and proclaim the gospel I was living as good news?

But pushing that red button was not the worst decision I made that fateful evening. The most catastrophic decision I made came immediately after I turned the television off.

I hurriedly dressed, rushed down to the front desk, and paid the movie charge myself—before my hosts would arrive to pick me up the next morning, check me out of the hotel, and pay for my room.

I destroyed the evidence.

And by doing that, I fashioned a mask for myself. A mask of strength. A mask of godliness.

A mask of lies.

I told myself I could take care of this. That I had it all under control. I told others nothing.

"How did you rest last night, Blaine?" my host asked me when we met up in the morning. And with my mask fully in place, I replied, "Had a great sleep! I'm ready to go!"

We went back to the event and preached a message hotter than a Walmart parking lot in July. The front swarmed with people who made commitments to God. What happened to me in that hotel room apparently had no impact on my ministry abilities; it certainly didn't quench the ability of the Holy Spirit to reach people through my anointed tongue as it spoke through the mask.

As I flew home to Tulsa that evening, I told myself, This would be the last time I ever do this. I committed my life afresh and anew to God. I would find a way to handle temptation the next time it snuck up. I spoke scriptures under my breath and reminded myself that God was bigger than any sin I needed to conquer. Together, He and I would kick this horrible thing out the door of my heart.

But I would never tell a soul.

Because I was a winner. I can beat this. And one more reason. I thought any confession of the horrible sin would mean the loss of everything. A national television show. The ability to provide for my wife and three children. My reputation and my future.

I could not take any chances. I can whip this. I just needed to pray more. Fast more. Read more. Believe more.

An interminable drumbeat of fear and self-loathing began to beat in my head. The slow death march had begun. And the band played a thousand lies.

Chapter Nine

SEXPERIMENTATION

It was something I never counted on.

My paddling into the porn pool would slowly lead me into a tidal wave of obsession with sexual fantasy. After my initial porn encounter in the hotel room, I thought for sure it would be the last. Surely the shame I felt in the months that followed would stay with me and be a constant reminder never to hit the little red button again. I went months … thinking everything was getting better … until another lonely night on the road … and the entire episode replayed again.

Same temptation. Different hotel. Same result. I gave in again. And from that moment forward, the times between my relapses into porn were not months, but weeks. And soon it would no longer be weeks, but days. I was caught in a cage that I couldn't get out of. I was still crying out to God for help … trying to figure out how to slay this deadly giant in my private world. I hated it. I hated what I was becoming. And I had no idea where it was going to take me.

The ancient Hebrew proverb perfectly described the insanity that was ahead of me: "Death and destruction are never satisfied, and neither are human eyes." (Proverbs 27:20)

One of my favorite writers, Eugene Peterson, interpreted this passage in *The Message* translation of the scripture like this, "Hell has a voracious appetite, and lust just never quits."

Lust (of any kind) unchecked can become an insatiable dragon of the heart that is continually leveraging your soul for a little bit more. One swiping claw at a time, it relentlessly demanded more.

More of my time.
More of my thoughts.
More of my energy.
More of my life.

What I'm about to tell you nearly scared the hell out of me. But sadly, not quite.

My cycle of porn—guilt—stopping—shame—and sinning again had gotten shorter and shorter. Then there was this hounding impulse to take the next step … to move out of the imaginary world of the mind into the real world of human contact.

"What would it actually be like to be with a real-life woman like the one I had lusted after on a hotel television screen?" was a question haunting my thoughts for months, until finally the perfect storm was set up one sultry night in Miami, Florida.

I was in Miami speaking and had a night off between engagements and of course I was sitting around bored in my hotel room alone. When I had checked in, my imagination began to run wild when I saw a strip club a few blocks away. Having traveled to nearly every major city in America, strip clubs were always easy to spot … bright neon lights everywhere, no windows, and all the ridiculous names … The Dancing Bare … Boobie Bungalo … seriously?

Unable to stop thinking about that club, I began to engage in a massive internal brawl between my heart and my head that was hell-bent with lust. The scripture calls it a war between the flesh and the spirit. My spirit was whispering, "No … you can't do this." Meanwhile my head screamed back … "You deserve a little relaxation … just check it out this one time and never go back again."

Someone once asked the question, "If two dogs of equal size and strength get in a fight, which one is going to eventually win?" The answer is simple, "The one you feed the most." I was feeding my "lust dog" nearly every day and my "spirit dog" was living on few kibbles and no bits.

So I went.

My heart was racing as I walked in the door. Somehow inside, I knew I was plunging into a new depth of sin. And I was overcome with fear that someone would recognize me. This was the first time I had ever gone public with my lust misdeeds. As I walked by the husky door bouncer into the club, there was the smell of spilled beer, loud music, dimly lit tables, and scantly clad women everywhere. There was nothing left to the imagination and for the first time, all the women were real. You could talk to them. You could touch them. And if you had a twenty dollar bill handy, you could dance with them.

I walked around the room for a few minutes taking in all the sights and eventually seeing how the routine worked. And I left. I couldn't do it. I felt so guilty … so completely horrible. I quickly walked out the door and jumped back in my rental car and raced to my hotel room. I prayed. I read my bible. I asked God for help.

I did everything except the one thing I should have done. Reach out to a trusted friend for help.

You might ask, "Wasn't God big enough … strong enough … to empower you to stop?" My answer will probably surprise you.

No. Not alone. God never created us to be islands. We were

made to live in a loving, healing, restorative community of friends and family. For me, that community is the church. We need each other to survive and yes, conquer the raging temptations and trials that we encounter in this out-of-control world.

That's why the scripture calls us to this community for strength.

Again, extracting a passage from Eugene Peterson's Message translation of scripture …

"Make this your common practice: Confess your sins to each other so that you can live together whole and healed. The prayer of a person living right with God is something powerful to be reckoned with"

James 5:16

Two hours after walking out of the club—I was back. Sitting at a table, I began drowning my fears and inhibitions with a couple bottles of beer. Eventually, I would yield to one of the many dancers who had come to my table inviting me to a private dance. And crash … I had taken one more step down the slippery slope into complete addiction … and destruction.

It wasn't long before I was in another city and ventured out again into a local strip club. I cautiously walked in, scanning the room for a table hidden in a corner of the room, and out of the shadows, this young man approaches me. He yelled over the pulsating music, "Hey, are you Blaine Bartel?"

My heart stopped.

He had recognized me from our television show. I was completely shaken and as I tried to maintain my composure, I simply looked up and said, "Yea man, that's me." And before he could ask me, I quickly asked him, "What are you doing here?"

He looked back at me with a hint of shame and replied, "I don't know man. I guess I shouldn't be here, right?"

Without even taking a second to think about it, I lied. Because that's what addicts do.

I quickly manufactured this contrived explanation that I was driving past this club and felt like the Lord told me to come in and "witness" to someone who needed the hear the gospel. I told him that maybe it was him I was supposed to help. I actually prayed for him and believe it or not, he thanked me.

We talked another thirty seconds and then I quickly sidled out as timid as a falling snowflake. To this day, I hate the out-and-out hypocrisy of that moment in my life. It was Blaine living his worst life now.

I cannot possibly describe the overwhelming shame and fear that I lived with the next several months. I woke up everyday thinking about this young man I met. "How had I compromised his faith in Jesus?" "Was he going to call our ministry offices and expose my double life?"

I never heard from that young man again. I had my first brush with possible exposure of my secret life and somehow I survived.

That day was coming. And there would be no escape.

Chapter Ten
WHEN THE FIRE DIES

I started *Fire by Nite* under the umbrella of a larger ministry led by a very gifted leader named Willie George.

Willie would eventually build one of the most influential churches in America, Church on the Move in Tulsa, Oklahoma. I met Willie ten years before at a conference he taught at my church in Canada. I admired his creativity and ingenuity. He was a strong leader, full of vision, and that inspired me. Not long after meeting him, he invited me to move to Tulsa, Oklahoma to create and lead an arm of his organization that targeted teenagers.

Willie had grown up with an extremely difficult home life, with an absent father and a mother who struggled with alcoholism. Early in his teen years, he gave his life to Christ and decided to live with his uncle, who was a Pastor in West Texas. Because he grew up with little love or affection in his childhood, Willie learned to be a survivor. He had a strong will and I think because he expected a lot of himself, he equally expected a lot of those who worked for him.

If an employee in his ministry performed well, he was generous and very supportive of them. On the other side of the coin, laziness, inconsistency and a lack of productivity was not tolerated. I thrived under his leadership because of this. I worked hard, had a keen business mind and knew how to make things happen.

Occasionally I would get a call to Willie's office for an ass-chewing, but I would take it like a man and make whatever corrections were necessary.

Willie became like a second father to me. He was like Moses with a Texas drawl. He treated me like a son. Though he was never known for his affection, every so often he would give me a huge bear hug and look me in the eye and say, "I sure love you Doc. I appreciate all you do." "Doc" was code for those Willie really respected. These moments made me feel like a million bucks.

However, after seven years of producing more than 90 programs of *Fire by Nite*, I was emotionally and spiritually ground into powder. I had lost my passion and many of the friends I had worked with on the program, had moved on to other things. Though I wouldn't admit it at the time, I had been overcome by sexual obsessions and believed that somehow a fresh start in life and ministry might be the cure to this ugly part of me that I despised.

With my nerves at an all-time high, I met with Willie, who was both my boss and Pastor, and I revealed my desire to move on to something new.

Well, to use some Texas slang, my news was about as welcome as a porcupine at a nudist colony. It didn't go over well.

He was not happy about it. I felt like the bad guy … that somehow I was disloyal and letting him down. But I reasoned in my head that I had given some of the best years of my life to him. I had helped bring millions of dollars into Willie George Ministries with video sales, a variety of other products, and conference income. Willie launched out on his own years ago—why couldn't I?

My pay ended abruptly, and I could feel the cold distance from all the other staff avoiding me in my final days in the office.

By this time, Willie had started Church on the Move and it

was now over 1,000 people. I had been the youth pastor during the first year of the church plant. So Willie brought us up on the platform to pray for us and give us an obligatory send off. The entire church rose to their feet, applauding for more than a minute. For a brief moment, my wife Cathy and I felt loved and extremely thankful. But reality was about to hit us square in the face.

My departure brought all kinds of fears to the surface.

At the time, the hottest act in Christian music was a one man show who was simply known as Carman. He was handsome and single, so women fawned over him and his Vegas-like persona was packing arenas across the country. He sold out Texas Stadium, former home of the Dallas Cowboys with 70,000 fans.

Carman had been a guest more than once on *Fire by Nite* and decided to start his own television show that was a carbon copy of ours. In fact, he hired our former director, the extremely talented Steven Yake, to put his show together. Carman's show was growing in popularity and was perceived as a threat to us at *Fire by Nite*.

Looking back, my departure gave Willie some legitimate concerns that *Fire by Nite* would lose its market share of video distribution to churches and homes. There was always the possibility that the FBN audience would not embrace a new host and that the production staff may not rally around it's newly crowned front runner, Eastman Curtis.

Fire by Nite would last one more year.

In that year, video distribution dwindled from 4000 monthly subscribers to under 1000. The program was canceled. Let me be clear. This was no fault of Willie George, Eastman Curtis or the staff that worked so hard on the program. Each and every one of them were extremely talented and capable. *Fire by Nite* had simply run it's course. As Ecclesiastes says, "There's a time to be born and a time to die."

45

By this time, Cathy and I had moved to Colorado Springs to plant a brand new church. I was also keeping a very hectic travel schedule to try to supplement our minimal salary in a fledgling church start up. The "fresh start" I was hoping for never materialized. My busy schedule only amplified my burned out state and now that I was no longer the popular TV host, many of the opportunities that role had afforded me were slowly drying up.

For the first time in my life, I was struggling with a sense of failure and loss. I began to question myself.

I felt alone in my private sinful world, and I was nosediving deeper and deeper into self hatred and longed for the days when I lived free from this awful vice. I seriously began to question if I could ever overcome it …

I would recite Psalm 51 again and again, reliving the Psalmist David's cry of repentance and yearning to experience the joy of my salvation that was now long gone.

Everything inside of me wanted to confess it and get it out of my life. I think deep down I knew that I would never win this battle alone. I had tried and failed too many times. I knew my sin was on a long term payment plan. Eventually the note would come due and utter destruction would be the payoff.

There were so many times I wanted go to Willie and say, "Pastor, I need help in getting free from this terrible stranglehold in my life!" So many have asked me, "Why didn't you just confess it, get it out in the open and get help?" I look back today with overwhelming regret, wishing I would have done just that. But at the time, both justification and fear paralyzed me.

I justified my sin by saying it wasn't really hurting anyone. It was a private battle … it wasn't affecting anyone else and one day, somehow … I would eventually beat my demons. I was a winner at everything I did … sports … relationships … ministry … I would eventually slay this giant too.

But fear was the greatest factor for keeping my secret shrouded. I had been a first hand observer of my own friends losing everything when their sexual sin was brought to light. And then there were the national scandals back in the day. Jimmy Swaggart. Jim Bakker. They lost everything.

I simply could not summon the courage to ask for help. I truly believe today Willie and many other friends would have helped through a recovery process if I had just asked.

But I didn't. And the grave I was digging for myself was about to get even deeper.

Chapter Eleven
A COLORADO CAUTIONARY TALE

Its snow covered summit represented a new mountain for me to climb.

Pikes Peak was only one of the postcard views in our new home in Colorado Springs. Moving to this beautiful city brought a new sense of energy in my soul. We were starting over in ministry. I would begin leveraging my popularity with young people and youth pastors into a national speaking trek called "The Young Revival Techno Tour." It was a multi-media message that I brought to churches, youth groups and conferences on the necessity for a revival of God's standards in our culture. The plan was to travel the nation for a year while we prepared to launch a new church in Colorado Springs.

It was also my chance for a new beginning in my soul.

No more porn. Leave all my sin behind in Tulsa. Like the snow covered peak that backdropped our beautiful new home, God would cover my sin with a fresh blanket of his forgiveness. I was always looking for "big moments" to finally put my private struggle with my sin behind me.

New Years Day.
My birthday.
Groundhog Day.

Anything really ... that would give me a some kind of mental momentum to finally find the will to change.

Surely relocation to another city and the responsibilities I would now bear in leading my own ministry would be all the impetus I would need to bury all my past shit. Before you get offended at that word, let me assure you that is exactly what it was to me. I hated it. Even the great Apostle Paul said that he counted all things but DUNG for the excellency of knowing Christ. Not sure if you know what dung is ... but it's shit today.

But it wouldn't be long before I found out that special occasions ... brand new cities ... even new relationships.. would never change what was on the inside on me.

My lustful addiction jumped in the car with me when I left Tulsa.

It was looming beneath the surface as I took our family to the top of Pikes Peak for the first time. It was still with me when I hit the road for the first leg of my speaking tour.

All I was able to do was keep it at bay during my new burst of enthusiasm and excitement. It wouldn't take long for the new shine of a new beginning to wear off. Within months of arriving in one of the most beautiful cities in America, the ugly monster inside was demanding to be fed again.

Shortly after landing in the Springs, I met a man who would have profound influence in my life. Ted Haggard was the pastor of one of the fastest growing churches in the nation. He would eventually become the President of the National Association of Evangelicals and would arguably carry more influence than any Christian leader in the country.

While preparing to launch our new church, Ted and his wife Gail kindly invited us to attend New Life Church. Ted had a different kind of vibe from most pastors. He didn't treat me as a competitor, but rather a colleague in the city. We met often and he was always an encouraging force in my life.

I had no idea that Ted was struggling with his own demons.

Several years later, he would be outed by a male prostitute named Mike Jones, with accusations of gay sex and drug use. Ted would fall harder than a 300 pound parachuter who couldn't find the rip cord. He lost everything in one week's time. He was removed from the church he had built from a couple of families to over more than 10,000 people. The overseeing pastors on his trustee board forced him to sign an agreement to leave the State of Colorado in order to receive a rather meager severance package to take care of his family's needs. He became a national punching bag in the media and on blog sites. Eventually HBO produced a documentary on Ted following him around with a camera as he tried to sell insurance to pay the bills.

I was flabbergasted.

One day he was visiting with President Bush in the Oval office. Now he is knocking on stranger's doors, hawking insurance.

I remember watching every moment of Ted's undoing on the national news and social media. My heart went out to him and his beautiful family. They had all sacrificed so much to build this amazing church and poof—it was gone.

Ted's story became a personal precursor for me. While I did not have near the national exposure that Ted had, his personal demise provided an ugly cautionary tale of how my world would end if my sin was ever exposed. I truly believed the church world would throw me away me like another dirty rag in a greasy kitchen.

Interestingly enough, Ted would ask me to join his staff team a few years later. I turned down his offer. We didn't talk again after that. Until one afternoon at a sex rehab center in Arizona, a future I was unaware of at the time.

Shortly after moving to Colorado Springs, I began to hire a staff team to help me carry out the work of this new assignment. I hired Jim Parton, who had worked with me in Tulsa with Willie George Ministries. He was my office manager and his wife Shawn helped Cathy with our three growing boys. An enthusiastic *Fire by Nite* fan named Erin who we met at New Life Church became our administrative assistant and it wasn't long before my sister Luanne and her husband Darryl moved from Canada to help us. When we launched our church a year later, my Mum and Dad moved from Canada as well to assist in all we were doing.

As our staff grew, so did my stress levels.

It was a constant struggle to make payroll every two weeks. I took a significant reduction in my previous income in order to sustain our new ministry operation. I knew going in that sacrifices would have to be made to get this new baby out of the crib and walking, but I had no idea what kind of mental and emotional toll it would take on me.

Darryl and I were traveling the nation in an old blue van perfectly packed with our tour equipment and product. We would drive several hundred miles each day, set up all the gear and merchandise, and I would preach like a house on fire that night, tear everything down, go out for a late dinner with our host pastor … and then do it all over again the next day. I was absolutely exhausted.

Questions and fears would mount in the months to come …

Did I make the right decision leaving Willie?
Was it always going to be this difficult to make ends meet?
Could I really make it on my own?

On top of this, my marriage to Cathy was suffering more and more. I was continually gone … sometimes for a month at a time. I remember trying to appease her constant appeals to work on our diminishing relationship by attending a marriage conference with her. Listening to the speaker, session after session, I remember thinking, this is impossible. You guys must be living in LaLa land or something! I don't have the time you have to sit around and write my wife love poems. And I'm sure as heck not home enough to do a "date night" every week. I couldn't wait for the damn thing to end.

However, simmering beneath the surface of my complaints was something much more consequential.

My love for porn had replaced my love for my wife.
And ministry had become my mistress.

Our next ministry trip would turn directions to the East Coast. I was booked to speak ten times in fourteen days. We desperately needed the income that would result from these meetings. And as it turned out, this leg of our tour would help a lot of people.

But it would kill me.

Chapter Twelve
SNAP

I looked out the window of the run-down Holiday Inn I was staying at somewhere in Pennsylvania. I had just arrived and was preparing to speak that night at a church. Beyond the smoke filled drapes in my window was a modest little building with a lackluster sign that immediately commandeered my attention.

Massage.
Thoughts began pin-balling through my head.

I deserve a good massage.
I wonder if they are open late?
What kind of massage is it?

Somehow, looking down from that hotel window, it had all the trappings of David catching a first glimpse at Bathsheba.

Like David, I was weary from battle. I felt a sense of entitlement. It wouldn't hurt to check things out and see what it is.

You see, I don't believe David started out thinking, "I'm going to commit adultery with that woman," as he looked down from his porch. The scripture says he began by simply sending messengers down to find out about her.

The deadly beginnings of our destruction often start with the notion of investigation or simple inquiry. We convince ourselves of the innocence of our "wonderings." And slowly, like a mouse following one morsel of cheese after another, it finally bites into the cheese deliciously baited in the trap.

And SNAP.

The trap was clearly there for the mouse to see. But its eyes are focused on one thing.

The cheese.

Arriving back at my hotel room after speaking that evening, I was drawn to the window again, this time to see the brightly lit sign on the otherwise dimly lit street.

Cheese.

I paced back and forth in my room contemplating a potential visit … my curiosity growing with each minute on what was on the other side of the door beneath that sign. Finally I told myself it's probably just a massage. Nothing more. What could possibly be wrong with that?

I was tired.
I was full of stress.
And moments later, I was pulling open that door.

An elderly Asian lady greeted me at the door. "You want massage?," she said in her broken English.

In a feeble attempt to resist saying yes, I replied uncomfortably, "How much?"

She responded quickly, "Forty dollars." I resisted again uttering, "How late are you open?"

She said, "Midnight … come in … I have very pretty lady for you."

My heart began thudding against my rib cage so loud, I could hear it. She had made it abundantly clear this was more than a just a massage. Finally, gathering every ounce of resolve I could find, I muttered, "Thanks, I was just checking." And I left. Walking back to my room, I felt like every demon in hell had descended upon my soul. I walked back to the hotel determined to go to bed, turn on a good movie and drift off to see another day.

Thirty minutes later, I was back.

Walking down the dingy hallway, an odor of cooked oriental food, scented candles and badly stained carpet filled my senses. It would be a smell that I would become very accustomed to in the years to come. Walking into a small room with a massage table and corner lamp, the elderly lady asked for my money, telling me to get undressed and lie on the table. Closing the door, she said that a girl would be with me shortly.

I laid down. Now my heart was beating harder than a snare drum at a metal concert. Finally, the door cracked open. "Hello?" I looked up to see an attractive and scantily dressed Asian girl, likely in her twenties.

As she began her massage, I tried to convince myself that this was all it was going to be. But this was no ordinary massage. With each passing moment, my mind and my senses were heading into overdrive. In the coming moments, I truly believe I felt every positive and every negative emotion in human existence all at one time.

Tranquility.
Fear.
Seduction.
Shame.
Pleasure.

Guilt.

Forty-five minutes later she looked into my eyes and then leaning over, she whispered into my ear, "What else can I do for you?"

Her words were like cyanide covered in candy.

SNAP.

You may remember one chapter ago, I told you this ministry trip would kill me. Allow me to explain. The concluding words of the seventh chapter of Proverbs is a sobering epilogue of a life given over to unchecked sexual impulses.

"I've spread fresh, clean sheets on my bed, colorful imported linens. My bed is aromatic with spices and exotic fragrances. Come, let's make love all night, spend the night in ecstatic lovemaking!

My husband's not home; he's away on business, and he won't be back for a month." Soon she has him eating out of her hand, bewitched by her honeyed speech.

Before you know it, he's trotting behind her, like a calf led to the butcher shop, Like a stag lured into ambush and then shot with an arrow, Like a bird flying into a net not knowing that its flying life is over.

So, friends, listen to me, take these words of mine most seriously. Don't fool around with a woman like that; don't even stroll through her neighborhood.

Countless victims come under her spell; she's the death of many a poor man. She runs a halfway house to hell, fits you out with a shroud and a coffin.

(Message Translation)

Looking back, I feel like this was a tipping point in my destructive path. Almost like there was no turning back. I was under an addictive spell. The shroud and the coffin had been fitted. My lust had become my death wish. It was just a matter of time.

But just when I thought it was over, a glimmer of hope pierced through my darkened world. Willie George invited me to come back to Tulsa. And together we would pull off something that had never been done in the history of the church.

Chapter Thirteen
ALL THAT YOU CAN'T LEAVE BEHIND

My nerves were red-lining like a tach in a new Corvette.

Would anyone show up? This is the greatest fear of any church planter on the first Sunday.

We had little start up money. We had no denominational backing and we didn't know a soul when we moved to Colorado Springs. I strapped on my guitar and led a chorus of worship songs in a small elementary school cafeteria, followed by an inspiring message outlining the vision of The Lord's Church. Well, I thought it was inspiring. Perhaps not. We had 119 men, women, boys and girls show up the first Sunday of the launch of a new dream.

The next week there were 56.

It felt like revival in reverse. People were staying away in droves. Didn't they know how popular I was? Why wasn't my success in television and my rock star status as a youth evangelist translating into a larger church explosion? I hated any scent of failure and this was starting to stink.

Any Pastor will tell you that they never see all the people who turn out each Sunday as much as they see the ones who didn't. Church planting is not for the faint of heart. You have to embrace the audacity to brave small crowds, lousy equipment, minuscule offerings, loopy visitors and continual self doubt—in hope of a better day.

It is a grind. But I pressed on. I've always been energized by the opportunity to build something out of nothing. For some reason, God gave me an ability to cast a vision for an extraordinary future that inspires followers to look beyond our pedestrian present.

Slowly, this motley group of Christians began to grow. We loved and embraced each person and family that came in the door. We had the good fortune of attracting a couple families that carried some significant influence in the city. One of the department leader's at Focus on the Family began to come with his family. Some of their friends would follow and gradually word began to spread about The Lord's Church in Colorado Springs.

Word got back to me that there were several Pastors in the city that were a little miffed with our name. How could we be "The Lord's Church?" They theorized that I was making a statement that we were the only church in town belonging to the Lord.

While that was far from the truth, I was kind of happy we were creating some buzz in the community, even if it wasn't with our less than amazing services.

Cathy would tell me later in life that our time in Colorado Springs was her favorite memory looking back. With both of us growing up in Calgary, Alberta, it felt a lot like home, being close again to the mountains. Jeremy, Dillon and Brock were all in their elementary school years and we introduced them to snowboarding and hockey in the winter, while climbing mountains and camping in the summer. And with my sister and brother-in-law, along with my Mum and Dad assisting as well, we had so much to be thankful for.

By now, Willie and I had mended our differences and he began to support our church plant with $1000 each month until we got our feet on the ground. A year later, we had grown to 200 people and moved into our own leased building right off Academy Boulevard, one of the busiest streets in the city. Willie came and preached our building dedication. It seemed like now that we were both pastors and on equal footing, our relationship was good.

It was now four years since moving to Colorado and everything on the surface seemed to be blooming like a mountain rose. Our church had grown to 450 people and we had bought twenty acres of land with plans to construct our own building. I had purchased the rights to *Fire by Nite* from Willie after the show had nosedived following my departure. We tried to resurrect the show in Colorado Springs but it was like General Motors trying to start over in a two car garage with three people. We simply didn't have the same talented cast of people both in front and behind the camera, nor did we have the budget.

However, Trinity Broadcasting Network paid us for the rights to air the program on their national Christian network. Everyone else on that network paid TBN handsomely for airtime. The fact that they paid us said a lot about the quality of our show back in the day. I can tell you this, the infusion of cash into our ministry helped us enormously at the time.

But beneath the rosy surface, I was struggling and unsettled. I was continuing to lose the battle to porn and sexual vice. The experience at the massage parlor seeded my curiosity and growing addiction. I began to scout out similar experiences in other cities. I would scan the yellow pages or a local entertainment tabloid looking for places that were usually ferreted out in the seedy part of town. Things were getting worse. Resistance was getting more and more futile.

And then the call came.

"Hello Pastor," I said with a warm voice. The next few minutes would change everything.

He began to describe a brand new student ministry that he had started at Church on the Move. He called it Oneighty—with the idea of turning students in a whole new direction—towards Jesus rather than the world. He went on to explain that four hundred teenagers were coming every Wednesday night, with lives being given to Christ each week. He described how the Lord instructed him to invest in the young people of his church personally. He was having his Associate Pastor teach the adults on Wednesday night and he was personally shepherding this new youth ministry.

This was unheard of. No pastor had ever made this kind of commitment to their church's teenagers.

And then he told me, "Blaine, I want to invite you and Cathy to come back. I want you to assume the leadership of Oneighty as our Student Pastor." He went on to tell me that he was committed to continue to invest his time and the church's resources to reach the entire city's teenagers. As he spoke, my imagination was going wild. This was the first time I had ever encountered a Lead Pastor with an all-out vision and pledge to reach young people.

He flew us into to Tulsa and we saw this brand new phenomenon first-hand. It was everything he described and more. The youth room was state-of-the art with decor and technology that looked like something out of Hollywood. And the students were so fired up. This was everything I had dreamed of.

I put my visionary mind into overdrive ... Willie and I had partnered to produce the most popular Christian television show for teenagers in America. What if we were used by the Lord to build the largest student ministry in the nation? Why not?

We told him we were coming. We announced our plans to move back to Tulsa to our church. While disappointed, most of our Colorado Springs congregation were supportive of our decision. We found a Pastor to take my place and within a few months we were back home at Church on the Move.

But once again, there was something deeper going on in my delight upon returning to Tulsa and leading the charge in this new vision to reach the young people of an entire city.

It may have been my final chance to leave my sin and lust behind. For good. And I did.

For six months.

Chapter Fourteen
THE CONTRADICTION CALLED ONEIGHTY

More than thirty buses rolled into the parking lot that night filled with teenagers of every stripe.

There was a line of cars extending all the way down 129th street—parents dropping off their kids at the front door of the largest student ministry center ever built in America. This $10 million dollar facility was a little piece of heaven on earth for teenagers who came from as far as seventy miles away every Wednesday night. It had an indoor glass-enclosed-basketball court, a movie theater-like cafe, Apple computer stations, a slew of video and arcade games, pool tables and a state-of-the-art auditorium.

Outside was a giant mountain of dirt with professional motocross jumpers sailing high above hundreds of wide-eyed onlookers. This would be our largest gathering ever. I would preach that evening to more than 3000 young people, with hundreds streaming forward at the end of my message to commit their lives to Jesus.

It was called Oneighty. And we made history.

One of our students actually came up with the name *Oneighty* and it signified turning away from the destruction of our sin and failure towards Jesus. We called it "doing a 180."

It became the largest local church student ministry in America. Our extraordinary 90,000 square foot facility was the envy of every youth pastor in America. We had pastors and church leaders that were coming from literally around the world to find out how we were reaching so many teenagers in Tulsa, Oklahoma of all places. Eventually we "franchised" the program and equipped more than a thousand churches around the globe to duplicate the ministry model we had produced.

National newspapers, news shows and magazines were coming into to Tulsa to interview us and cover the "happening" called Oneighty. A call even came from Jon Stewart's *The Daily Show* requesting an opportunity to come and interview us. We wisely turned them down, knowing their penchant for making everyone they interview look dumber than a sack of wet mice.

The number one question people asked me was, "What is the magic ingredient to Oneighty's blockbuster results?"

My immediate answer was that it was something The Lord has orchestrated because He loved young people so much. And I still believe that to be true. But it seems God chooses to use people in His work. And looking back there were a lot of wonderful people that made Oneighty happen. Our amazing staff and interns to start with. I wish I could tell you about every single one of them. But the one young man that had the most significant impact on our internal operations was my assistant student pastor and life-long friend, Erik Lawson. Erik and I were brothers-in-arms and our success story had his fingerprints all over it. Today, Erik pastors a large church in St. Louis and I am so proud of him.

I also have to give major props to my wonderful friend, Lee Wilson. Lee is a strong, black "Jesus man" whom the Lord saved in the projects of Houston, Texas. After graduating from high school, he showed up in my life when I was still doing *Fire by Nite*.

He knew how to rap and make people laugh, so I took him all over the country with me reaching teenagers. Lee masterminded our Urban 180 Saturday morning outreach, which bussed in nearly one thousand young people from the poor and most neglected parts of our city. A good majority of these kids were black and trying to find hope in a very difficult existence. Lee and his team understood their stories and spoke into their lives with incredible grace and compassion.

There were also the hundreds of volunteers that served every single week. Our ushers, greeters, security team, hospitality workers, school campus leaders, bus drivers, maintenance people and all the parents who opened up their hearts and homes to our small groups, made our entire operation click. I think of Dr. Richard Presley and his wonderful family who helped round up as many as four hundred students weekly, transporting them to Oneighty every Wednesday night. People like Johnny Hampton, Chris Munch, David and Sammye Rogers, Mark and Chana Keefer and Viccijo Witty also come to mind … especially in the formative years of our ministry. There were so many more and I loved every one of them.

But the creators of Oneighty were Pastor Willie George, his son Whitney George and myself. Building the Oneighty brand and operation was a family venture.

Pastor George was the Father. It would have never happened without his guidance and resources. He championed thousands of Church on the Move members to get behind this ministry and support it with both their time and money. And I don't know any other prominent pastor that would have done this … Willie canceled the national television show he was paying to broadcast all over the country and threw all of that money and energy into building his youth group.

Whitney was the son. Whit was Pastor George's oldest boy and had a very unique and innovative spirit, with a splash of youthful hubris. He was the key member of my Oneighty staff team and there was nothing he wasn't good at. He was a genius thinker, a talented graphic designer, a pretty good musician and singer—but more than anything, Whit had his father's ear. Willie trusted his son and Whit used his sway with Dad to continually push us to explore new frontiers (and spend more money) to reach young people.

In the 80's, I was Whit's children's pastor, in the 90's, I was his youth pastor and now we were working side by side making youth ministry history. Today Whit has assumed the role of Lead Pastor from his father at Church on the Move and he has grown into an extraordinary man and leader.

I suppose I was big brother. I was the one with boots on the ground rallying and equipping the troops each week to make the entire operation happen. That included organizing more than thirty campus ministries, a fleet of forty buses and drivers, writing manuals and messages, coordinating security, training three hundred plus volunteers, stopping gang fights, dealing with angry parents, leading our conference ministries … on and on … you get the picture. I was busy. But I loved it.

The first six months of our return to Tulsa, I was fueled by the new momentum in my life to avoid returning to massage parlors, though pornography was still an occasional outlet in my life. But as the writer of Proverbs so colorfully describes, I eventually re-engaged in my folly, just as a dog returns to his vomit.

It was during this time that I encountered one of the most difficult moments in my life as a father.

One spring afternoon, I walked into our game room to discover my middle son Dillon watching porn on our family computer. Complicating this terribly awkward moment even more, was this. It was gay porn. Of course, Dillon was embarrassed and began to apologize profusely. My response back was a toxic emotional cocktail of anger and shame towards him. Yet on some level, I was projecting the very anger and shame I felt for my own sin on my precious child.

Dillon was an extraordinary kid growing up. He had a genuine love for people, especially the underdog. He was every teacher's favorite student and one of the most popular kids at Lincoln Christian School, Church on the Move's private school, where each of our boys attended. Dillon was especially favored by the girls, but was teased and bullied by some of the tough kids on campus. Names like "queer" or a "fag" would find their way to his ears. Dillon had a very tender side to him and he loved gymnastics, which enabled him to be one of the best male cheerleaders on the school cheer team. So here's what a fall Friday night looked like for the Bartel family. Brock playing defensive back. Dillon cheering his team on. Jeremy filming the game. And Mom and Dad screaming from the stands.

I didn't know what to think about Dillon. What was going on in his life? Was he gay? How could I possibly help him? I was completely screwed up myself. As his father, I felt responsible for all of it. Somehow or some way ... had my sin opened the door for immorality in our home? The hardest thing in the world was having "the conversation" with him. When I asked him why he looking at these websites, he assured me through an unending stream of tears that he was just exploring different kinds of sites and would never do it again. I just hugged my son and prayed with him for forgiveness.

And I felt like a complete sham of a father.

Cathy and I took him to a highly recommended Christian counselor in Tulsa and about three months later, he told us Dillon was on the right track, doing great and that this episode in his life was just a brush with teenage curiosity. We were relieved to say the least. Dillon was A-OK.

Right.

With that crisis solved, I could get back to running Oneighty, racing around in my Porsche 911 and savoring my new status as America's most prominent student pastor. By now I had developed a monthly audio coaching club that had more than a thousand subscribers. I had also written a best-selling book series for students, including the most popular title in the series, "Every Teenager's Little Black Book of Sex and Dating." Who better to teach kids about moral purity, right? I was also hitting the leadership conference circuit as a keynote speaker at some of the largest Christian events in the country. We had a sprawling new house and property, a stack of money in the bank and I was rubbing shoulders with some of the most influential leaders in Christendom.

But trust me when I say that the irony of me leading "Oneighty" was not lost on me. It seemed like I was stuck on the "360" merry-go-round. As much as I would try to turn my life around privately, I would always find myself right back where I started.

I woke up everyday.
I looked in the mirror.
And with disdain and sadness softly hissed, "I hate you."
My curiosity had become a habit.
My habit had become an obsession.
My obsession had become an addiction.

And unknown to me, my addiction was a crouching tiger, just waiting for the perfect moment to take me down.

The tiger would finally bear it's fangs and strike.

In a city called Dallas.

Chapter Fifteen
BLAINE DOES DALLAS

Not long ago, I took the Enneagram Personality Test, a forced-choice psychological evaluation that is one of the few personality tests that got it right with me. My primary trait was that of The Enthusiast. The results described me as playful, high-spirited, optimistic and constantly seeking new and exciting experiences.

On the flip side, these characteristics can easily lead to impulsiveness, impatience and complete exhaustion. Wow—talk about taking a long look in the mirror. I've always been that guy. You know, the one that wants the shiny new object. I was susceptible to anything that looked new, exciting and challenging that came along.

I remember stopping our rented van on our family Disney vacation at the sight of people jumping off a huge construction crane with a bungee cord strapped to their ankles. I had to try it. What could be better than jumping head first towards a concrete parking lot from a random piece of machinery? On another vacation in Hawaii, I came within a breath of drowning while trying to body surf the treacherous North Shore.

This unappeasable quest for challenge and even danger would set me up for the next thirty-six months of my life that I am just going to call "the insanity years."

After leading the charge for Oneighty for seven years, I was ready for something new. I turned the reigns over to my capable assistant, Erik Lawson and Pastor George invited me to be his assistant Pastor at Church on the Move. *Note: The reason I refer to him as Pastor George now and not Willie is simply because of his change of roles in my life. Early on, he was more like a mentor and boss. But now he was my pastor and it was a part of the honor code to refer to him as Pastor George.

After nearly three years in my role as assistant Pastor, I was beginning to feel a yearning to lead my own church. I was being asked to preach at least once a month to the adult congregation at Church on the Move and I was always warmly received by our people. I was repeatedly complimented for my creative sermons and my insightful sense of humor. In addition to speaking, I learned on the fly how to operate a mega-church of 10,000 people. From the counseling to the army of volunteers, it all fell under my leadership.

In our department head meetings with Pastor George, we had talked and prayed about starting a church in Dallas one day. Pastor George was from Texas and for all of us small city Tulsa folk, Dallas was just four hours away and it was big time. But the idea never really went anywhere.

Until one unforgettable weekend in Chicago.

Whit and his younger brother Gabriel, along with myself and some other staff members were attending a Willow Creek Arts Conference. Willow Creek Church is one of the largest and most progressive churches in the nation. Hundreds of thousands of pastors and church leaders have migrated there to discover new ways of "reaching those who are far from Christ." (one of Willow's common slogans) While attending this conference, I had a sudden urge to pray. I went back to the hotel room that afternoon, lit some candles, (a custom during my extended prayer times) and began to wait on the Lord. I had a deep sense that now was the time to plant a church in Dallas and that I should talk to Pastor George when I got home.

Then this happened. Pastor George's younger son Gabriel, pulled me aside later that evening and said, "Blaine, if you ever go to Dallas to start a church, I want to go with you and help." Wow. I was floored. Perhaps God was orchestrating something much bigger than anything I had ever dreamed of. Gabe and I were quite close and he had a flair for design and graphic arts, as well as a huge heart for children's ministry. He and his wife, Sommer, would be perfect on our church planting team.

When I look back now, I have to ask myself, "Was it really the Lord leading us to Dallas to plant a new church community?" If so, why would He call me to do this, given the state of my soul and the unbreakable bondage to lust I was warring with? To be honest, I really don't have the answer for that. I know God has always used broken and marred people.

Jonah was a rebel.
David was an adulterer and murderer. Peter was a betrayer.

Perhaps He was giving me a final opportunity to get me to a place to finally find help. Because, as the future would play out, those opportunities would come in ways I could never imagine.

Five months after that hotel room prayer, we were moved to Dallas with a team of people, including Gabe and Sommer, as we prepared to launch Northstar Church. Pastor George and Church on the Move had graciously given us complete financial support for the first year of our start up. We decided to plant our new community in the northern suburb of Frisco, which was the fastest growing city in America in 2006. There were new families moving into this hot new destination every day and most were looking for a church. Frisco was home to the Dallas Stars practice facility, which wasn't lost on this Canadian boy. Within a year, we had a Dallas Star alumni, Bobby Bassen, coming to our church and I was so excited to be able to share my love of hockey with Bobby, who would become a good friend.

We launched our church and had about two hundred people coming in the first month. Three years later, we raised enough money to build a five million dollar building on Legacy Drive, which was one of the main parkways in Frisco. When we moved out of our temporary digs at Embassy Suites into our very modern new home, our congregation spiked from 400 to 800 in just a few months. We were on the watch list with several church growth experts in the nation, pointing to Northstar Church as a future mega-church. We were already preparing to launch a second location in the historic Lakewood Theater, not far from Southern Methodist University and the hip lower Greenville area of Dallas.

God had given us a wonderful staff team. Steven Pritt was one of our best Oneighty leaders and was overseeing our volunteers. Chris Lindberg was killing it as our student Pastor. Joshua Blount was one of my Oneighty students and joined us to lead our children's ministry. Betty Hales was our administrative assistant, who also moved from Tulsa, having been my executive assistant at Church on the Move. And John Goebel was overseeing our worship team and facilities.

Our family seemed to be doing better than ever too. Cathy was enjoying being a Pastor's wife and pouring her heart into the ladies of our church, and they all loved her. She is one of the most caring and loving individuals you will ever meet. And she has always been an extraordinary mother. Jeremy had tracked down a great job as a video/film director at one of Dallas' top production houses, Charlie Uniform Tango, and Dillon was teaching gymnastics at Little Gym and making music. Brock was a senior at Wakeland High School.

Brock and I have always been super tight. Maybe because he was such a good athlete and we grew up playing sports together … or perhaps it was just that we have similar personalities—

carefree and spontaneous. I loved going to his football games on Friday nights. He earned the position of starting defensive back in his 4A Texas high school and that was an accomplishment for a skinny white boy from Tulsa. I was so proud of him.

I will never forget the time Brock was invited to participate in an inner city football camp in Deion Sanders' back yard in Prosper, Texas. Yes, his back yard. The former Dallas Cowboy Hall of Famer had a full length football field on his expansive estate and loved coaching young people. Deion called Brock "Sehorn," a flattering reference to the white stand-out defensive back for the New York Giants. (Brock was one of the only white kids on the field) One afternoon, I came by to watch Brock at practice and Deion yelled over to me, "Hey, Sehorn's Dad!!" Made my day … and my chest swelled with pride as I watched Brock run his drills.

Life was truly good. Our church was growing. Family was great. I had finally put my past behind me.

Until one hot summer day in August.

Chapter Sixteen
WHERE THE END BEGINS

Her name was Dakota.

A seductive blonde in her thirties, she worked in a Dallas massage studio that I visited a several times in my past visits to Dallas. Let's just say she knew me on a first name basis. By the way—that name was Curtis and not Blaine.

I couldn't get her out of my head.

It had been an entire year since I had been to a massage parlor or sex establishment of any kind. When we decided to move to Dallas I told myself (once again) that I had to stop my sin. A lot of people were counting on me and I truly believed we were about to embark on something very special. No more of this crap in my life. I still would have occasional relapses into porn, but in my mind that was the better of two evils.

You would think after resisting this crippling sin in my life for an entire year, that I had finally conquered my demons. Not even close. I was white-knuckling … teeth clinching … high-anxiety-ing … my way to abstinence.

Every. Single. Day.

I felt like a mountain climber hanging on to a small piece of jagged rock with one hand for dear life, dangling on the side of a thousand foot cliff.

I wasn't falling.
But I had no idea.
How much longer.
I could possibly hold on.

Driving my decked out F-150 down Highway 75 in Dallas, my eyes suddenly caught a very familiar exit sign—the one for Dakota's massage studio. My thoughts began to race out of control with memories of past visits. It was like a movie teaser in my head that I couldn't stop from playing. My heart was literally beating out of my chest and a massive hit of dopamine was exploding in my brain—I was flush with the thoughts of re-living the experience again.

"No, dammit! You can't do this Blaine!!"

One hour later, I walked out of that studio, a couple hundred dollars poorer and my head hung in shame. I had parked a block away to make sure no one I knew would see my truck parked in front of the studio. It was the longest walk of my life. All the work of resistance for the last year … gone in sixty minutes. I had given in again. I can't even begin to explain how unwinnable my battle felt at that moment.

And in reflection, I think I just tapped out. Like the MMA fighter surrendering to a choke hold and patting his opponents back, I knew I had been beat. This shit was way, way, way … stronger than me. Way … stronger. I had given it my best shot and come up short. Again. "F*CK. F*CK. F*CK." I'm sorry, that's the only way to accurately recount my self-directed rage.

I was a broken man. So completely lost.

The next three years, I would go stark raving mad. I believe I may have been subliminally ready to get caught or get killed. I started taking all kinds of risks and in some way, turned myself over to the devil. Take me Satan. Do what you want with me. Destroy me if you must. I deserve whatever comes my way.

I began to spend every waking moment on the internet. Searching escort sites and sex establishments everywhere I would go but especially in Dallas. There were sites for the Dallas area that had more than hundreds of women to choose from. It was like a shopping catalogue for sex. And I was spending thousands of dollars every single month now.

By now, I had created a secret identity in order to conceal my real life in the sexual underground I was endlessly exploring. My fake name was Curtis McKenzie. I had fake social media sites, complete with a fake bio and resume. I had a phony identification and a secret cell phone to make all my calls. I insisted on handling all of our family finances and made sure that Cathy could never track how much money we really had or how I was spending it. I had become desperate, devious and delusional.

Lying and deception became completely normal to me. I was the poker player at the table that had no tells. And a hand full of queens. I was constantly manufacturing reasons for leaving the house for protracted periods of time, so I could slip underground. I would create fake speaking engagements and then hole up in a Dallas hotel for three days, hooking up with women. Some were escorts and others through my fraud dating site profiles. And some just women I met in the bar. It didn't matter who it was or how it happened … it was all about the hunt and the prey.

I had become a hyper-narcissist, bordering on sociopathic.

And it was just a matter of time before my alternate world would begin to unravel.

I was taking random women I would meet to places like New

York or Los Angeles for weekend trips. My gluttonous appetite for lust and adventure kept pushing me to dangerous new limits. One night I was mugged by three men as I was walking into a club with a woman I had met in a seedy part of Dallas. They took my wallet and might have killed me if the woman I was with hadn't screamed as loud as she did.

The only thing that was off limits with me was ever having an "affair" with someone in my real world. You know—my church, family and friends world. There was no virtue in this boundary for me. It was pretty simple. I was never seeking a relationship with another woman. The only thing I was seeking was the gratification of my own lust. Period.

The end was getting closer and closer.

One of the escorts that had become a "regular" saw one of my credit card receipts and figured out who I really was. She tried to blackmail me for thousands of dollars. What did I do? I told her I had recorded our phone conversation and was going to turn it over to the police and prosecute her for extortion. There was always a way out. But the terror of being caught began to stalk me like a bad-tempered ghost in a haunted castle.

The only thing more formidable than the sheer terror of being caught, was my overwhelming obsession with lust. It was so consuming, that there were times I would meet up with four different women in one day. My days were spent in one of three ways: 1) Setting up encounters. 2) Meeting women. 3) Covering my tracks. By now, porn wasn't even on my radar. I was booking actual porn stars for sexual encounters. Who needed fantasy when the real thing was being sold online?

I was living out the refrain of Israel's famed King Solomon:

"I denied myself nothing my eyes desired; I refused my heart no pleasure. My heart took delight in all my labor, and this was the reward for all my toil."

Ecclesiastes 2:10 New International Version

I was living in the same dark and deceptive entitlement as this King. I had worked hard for what I had. I was being emotionally taxed trying to plant a new church. By now my marriage was in shambles. There was no intimacy. (because marital intimacy couldn't possibly live up to my fantasy world)

So guess what? I deserved this reward for all my toil and trouble. So I rationalized.

Even as I type these words, sharing the absolute worst part of my past with you, my heart breaks all over again. Tears are steaming down my cheeks right now. How did I become this person?

What was I thinking? How could I possibly come home, hug my unsuspecting wife, look her in the eyes and lie again and again? How could I continue to pretend to be the father and the hero that my three beautiful sons believed in and looked up to? And my Mom and Dad. Each time I would see them, they would go on and on about how wonderful a son I was and all that the Lord was using me to do. How could I look back at my own parents who had loved me so well, nod my head in agreement, while my heart was screaming, "You god-damned con artist!"

I believe we can come to a point when our sin turns into iniquity. What's the difference? The psalmist David, who was addressing his own sexual sins and failure, said this:

"Then I acknowledged my sin to you and did not cover up my iniquity."

Psalm 32:5 New International Version

The biblical definition of sin is "missing the mark." Iniquity in the Hebrew is *awon* and means "to bend, twist, distort." I believe there came a time in my continually choosing to act out in my sexual sin that my heart and mind became bent, twisted and distorted. I moved from committing evil acts to actually being evil.

In the final days of steady descent into more and more depravity, my mind was going places that were frightening. I had become extremely depressed … and dangerous. I was continually entertaining two scenarios that would end my horrible existence. The first was whenever I would be driving home from one of my clandestine meetings, the feelings that would immediately surface after my sinful acting out were self-hatred and shame. I would pick out one of the huge metal expressway standards and start driving towards it in a suicidal rush of emotion, often coming within inches of ending my life.

The second script that would play in my mind was an ill-conceived plan to secretly leave the country, move to somewhere in South America and start a new life. Have a do-over. Oh, to have that chance. If only I could leave it all behind. I was as deluded as OJ Simpson in his white Bronco and his $9,000 cash, fake mustache, passport and gun on his way to the border.

As fate would have it, there was a third scenario. But it played out in real time. It began in the wee morning hours of Monday, March 29th, 2010 would bring life as I knew it to a crashing end.

An innocent young lady whom I had deceived and become just another "throw away" in the wake of my sexual conquests, stared me down and through the pain of her betrayal announced, "I know who you are." And then her voice intensified, "And I'm stopping you from ever doing this again."

It was here.
The one moment I feared most. Was now upon me.
And this time, there would be no escaping.
Death was at the door.

Chapter Seventeen
48 HOURS OF PURGATORY

I remember it being a sunny Sunday morning in March.

In fact, it was Palm Sunday. As I closed our service at Northstar Church, I invited Cathy to join me on stage to pray for marriages in our swelling congregation. I didn't do this often. To be flat honest, I hated even talking about marriage, because of the private mockery I was making of my own. As I wrestled through the words of my prayer, Cathy would later tell me that this rare moment injected some brief ray of hope into her soul. "Maybe the Lord was going to begin a new work in our marriage," she mused with just enough optimism to push her on to another lifeless week of being wed to yours truly.

I hugged Cathy and Brock goodbye after our service and jumped in my truck for the airport and another speaking engagement. Well, that was the official story. I was actually on my way to a Dallas hotel. I checked in and grabbed a drink out of the minibar to loosen up. It was time to concoct a new adventure for the night to come. After a flurry of online searches, texts, emails and private messages, I finally settled on a woman I had been with on previous occasions.

It would be the most fate-filled decision of my life. But honestly, at this point, it was just a matter of time.

Her name was Cynthia.

She was a single mother I had lured into a sexual relationship on a dating site. Of course, my profile was on the site and was a fraud. I told her I was an author and single man with a son at home from a previous marriage. I gave her every indication that I cared for her and was truly interested in having a long term relationship, when all I wanted was another X-rated adventure.

I had broken my own cardinal rule with Cynthia. Never see a woman from a dating site more than two times. My reasoning was this: I didn't want her (or myself) to become emotionally involved. It was too risky. And the more time I would spend with someone, the more questions they would ask. My lies were like Ikea furniture—they set up nicely on the showroom floor, but would only hold up so long.

Here's how everything went down. We met for a few drinks at a bar near her house. During our conversation, she began asking me an inordinate amount of questions about my past. It made me a little nervous but I pushed past my concerns and we drove to her place. However, the rest of the evening she was unusually disinterested in any kind of romance. It didn't make any sense. She seemed fine at the bar. Her demeanor had completely changed. My fear antenna sky high. Was she on to me?

"I just need to get out of here," I thought.

After watching a movie together, with no hint of affection, I finally pushed off her large overstuffed couch and explained that I was dog-tired and going to head home. It was just past midnight when I sped away in my truck from East Dallas back to my hotel room near the Galleria Shopping Center.

With a deep sense of relief that I had gotten out of there unscathed, I vowed to never see her again. She was an extremely intelligent person and I just knew she was beginning to see through my carefully constructed mask.

Ten minutes later, my cell phone lit up. It was her. Oh no … what now? "Hey," I answered apprehensively. Her tone had completely changed. Now gushing with warmth, her soft voice beckoned me back, "Curtis, I am so sorry. I just had a back-breaking day at work. Please come back and spend the night with me. I need you."

Relief came over me. Everything was OK. Like a deer lured into an ambush, I reversed course and hit the accelerator back to her house. She met me on her front porch with the biggest smile.

She flirted, "I want to remember this night forever," and held her smart phone back to take a picture of the two of us together.

Before I could stop her, the flash went off.
She had her evidence.
And.
My heart fell out of my chest.

I knew I was caught.

She stepped back from me and called my bluff. I was out of aces and I had finally used up all the queens. She angrily described how she had plotted with the server at the bar, who was a friend of hers. The server had asked me for my ID and passed on my real identity to Cynthia. Now she had my name and knew I was conning her. But she waited until I left to Google it and find out exactly who I really was.

Of course, her search produced a dearth of links. My church. My book publisher. My blog site. My Facebook page. And hundreds of articles and photographs.

Not unexpectedly, she was in complete shock and outrage. Her ultimatum was clear. Confess or she would take me down.

Finally being recognized and exposed for who I really was brought me cascading down to the worst reality I have ever experienced. I had nightmares about this day. No, I mean I really had nightmares. I can't tell you how many times I dreamed of get- ting caught in my sin, only to wake up the next morning in sheer relief that my secret was still safe.

It was safe no longer.

I knew I was about to die. I had finally been cornered into a confession. Though it would not happen until later that week, the death of everything I had … everything I valued … all that I worked for … was coming. Yet, I just had to wait for it. Life was over for me, but it would take 48 hours to get there.

Why 48 hours?

Because I had something left that I had do. You would think it was impossible, but I did it. It was haunting and surreal.

You see I was scheduled to speak at a large youth conference in Amarillo, Texas the next day. My first inclination was to call my friend who was hosting it and cancel. But the pure madness that was filling my head almost dared me do it. So I boarded my flight in the morning and showed up as scheduled.

I didn't get even one wink of sleep the night before and I was in a daze the entire day.

Standing in worship that evening, just moments before I would be introduced to speak, tears began to escape my bloodshot eyes. I knew this was going to be final sermon of my life. The last time I would ever feel the unexplainable sense of bliss that comes when you have helped other people in their search for meaning.

But there was one more "last time." This would be the last time I would be introduced to an audience without an ugly stain on my good name and reputation.

When I took the stage, it was like I was transported out of my reality and into a holy cocoon for one final hour of bliss. I preached like there was no tomorrow. Because for me, there wasn't a tomorrow. This was it. More than a hundred young people streamed to my altar invitation to give their lives to Jesus. As I led them in a prayer for salvation, I couldn't help but think that I should be the one praying this prayer. Not leading it.

When I got back to my hotel room, I broke down in tears again. I truly believed I had just been used by God to speak into the hearts of people for the very last time. And I was going to miss it.

I would miss the feeling of the Holy Spirit working through me, bringing words and thoughts to my mind that people needed to hear. Watching hurting hearts respond to my sermon … falling to their knees in broken surrender to Jesus. And knowing I had a part to play in what God was doing in their lives.

How could I have been so stupid? To throw it all away for my selfish lust and pleasure? Every last ounce of lust and pleasure had now permeated into anger and shame.

Anger at myself. For failing one more time. Because I told myself the last time was the last time. And of course it never is.

Shame because I was the worst human being on earth. I believed that. I hated myself and I was quite sure by now, God hated me too. My life narrative had changed. I was no longer the David I had always wanted to be. The man that was after God's own heart. I had become the Philistine and there was a fatal rock coming for my head. And I deserved it.

I would stay up until 4:00am that Tuesday night. Smoking cigarettes in the hotel parking lot. Brooding about the day to come.

Tomorrow would change everything.

Scene Two

THE CRASH

"Like a lumbering boulder rolling down a hill,
truth will win out in spite of man's opposition.
It may be hindered, but it is impossible to stop."

—Anonymous

Chapter Eighteen

THE FORTUNATE DEATH
OF CURTIS MCKENZIE

I lifted my shade, squinting through the morning sun out my airplane window at the sprawling Dallas/Ft. Worth metroplex.

I had an epiphany. I was just another human being in a huge mass of seven million other human beings. Who was I, really? How could God possibly keep track of us all? I was landing in a city full of hurting people, lost people, poor people, lonely people … and loathsome people.

Evil lowlifes who had got away with murder.
Racists who justified their hate.
Parents who had abandoned their children.
Men who had raped women.
Greedy CEOs who had taken advantage of the poor.
Government racketeers who loved their bribes.

The nature of being human in this corrupt world kicked in. I was better than most of the evil rabble of this world. Why should I go down? My mind began to scramble for solutions …

How could I manage this situation? What could I do to limit the damage? I could offer Cynthia money for her silence. Or I could concoct a story of this being a one-time lapse in judgement.

Being an insider in so many evangelical ministry circles, trust me that I've been privy to more than my share of preachers who have covered up behavior that would make Madonna blush. There had to be a way out.

But in the end, I guess, I was just ready for it all to end. This was my one and only chance to leave the man behind that I had come to despise.

Curtis McKenzie had to be killed.

Nothing less than a full-throated confession would suffice. Exiting the Love Field airport, my first stop was to meet with Cynthia's pastor, Scott Camp. She asked me to meet with him before doing anything else. I agreed. He was waiting at the front of his church when I arrived. We sat in his office. He told me he knew who I was and had followed my ministry over the years. Through a deluge of tears, I told him everything. Scott was gracious and genuine. He put his arms around me, prayed for me and encouraged me to follow though on my disclosure to my family and church.

My next stop was Garden Valley, Texas, a modest East Texas community and the home of Teen Mania Ministries. Usually pushing my speed at least ten mph over the limit, today was different. My journey was slow, and my heart was pensive. No music. No talk radio. Complete silence. I was a zombie. The driving dead.

Ron Luce, President of Teen Mania, was still one of my closest friends in all the world. He also served on our church board of trustees. If there was anyone in this world I felt like I could trust with my secrets, it was Ron. And I had confidence in him to guide me through disclosure to my family and church.

Arriving, I walked into the Executive Office area and asked to meet with Ron. The receptionist warmly greeted me, having been there to speak many times and walked me back to Ron's office. I slumped down into a conference table chair. Moments later, Ron entered the room in his usual upbeat way … "Hey Blaine! How are you doing man? Great to see you!!"

As the afternoon sun shimmered through the corner office windows, my countenance betrayed me. Looking into my eyes, Ron knew immediately this would not be one of our normal meetings. There would be no dreaming about changing the world and no planning for the next great event that would reach thousands of teenagers. There would be no small talk either.

Nothing could prepare him for what was next.

As I started to speak, a torrent of tears flooded my eyes. The massive damn I had built in my life, that kept every single person in my life at a safe distance … broke. Tears began to form in Ron's eyes, and he didn't even know what this was about. But he could tell it was tragic.

I spent the next hour divulging everything. The porn. The 900 numbers. The massage parlors. The strip clubs. The escorts. The pick ups. The uncontrollable addictive, ugly, sinful, detestable stronghold that I had tried to break a thousand times. Only to fail again a thousand times more.

He listened solicitously to the entire crushing chronicle of my miserable cloak-and-dagger life. And then he reached down and pulled me out of my chair, wrapping his arms around me … and wept. He prayed fervently over my dead soul. Then he took me to his home, where I would spend the night, before returning to Dallas the next day.

Left alone in the house for a couple hours, I was drawn to the piano in the spare room. You see, Teen Mania had purchased their ministry property from Last Days Ministries, an outreach of the late Keith Green. Keith was my all-time favorite Christian music artist. He had died tragically in a plane accident on his ministry property in 1982. His songs were heart-rending and called the church to repentance from a lukewarm heart. I had listened to his song, "Asleep in Light" a thousand times in my reoccurring states of remorse, repentance and brokenness …

"The world is sleeping in the dark, That the church just
can't fight, 'cause it's asleep in the light!
How can you be so dead?
When you've been so well fed.
Jesus rose from the grave,
And you …
You can't even get out of your bed!"

The piano was Keith Green's personal piano. And I was in Keith and Melody's former home. Ron and his wife Katie had purchased it when they bought the ministry property. I felt like I was on holy ground.

Keith was much more than a singer to me. He and Melody lived the kind of Christian life I dreamed of living. They opened their home to the poor. They shunned the Christian music industry and gave their albums away. They served on mission fields. There was no sacrifice too great for the cause of Christ.

He was a hero to me. As I walked over to the instrument he had used to fill auditoriums around the world with the praises of Christ, all I could think about was the example he had set … and how short I had come in living out the message he had died for. I had learned one of Keith's songs years ago and sitting down on his piano bench, I began to play it.

It was most surreal moment. Looking up, I whispered, "Keith, if you can hear me. I'm sorry. I'm so sorry."

As I put my head on my pillow later that evening, I prayed tomorrow would never come.

Chapter Nineteen

BOMB RADIUS

We don't get to schedule the consequences of our lives. The truth is there are no secrets—only realities yet to be revealed.

The repercussions of my choices showed up at the worst possible time. It was just a few days before Easter, the biggest Sunday we would ever have at Northstar Church.

As Ron and I arrived in Frisco, we drove by our beautiful new church building on Legacy Drive, which was just blocks away from our home. Huge signs out front welcomed the community. I dropped my head in lament as we motored by.

I don't know why, but I have always wondered what kind of fear a suicide bomber faced moments before they walked into a crowded market with explosives wrapped around their body knowing they were about to blow up everyone within a hundred feet to kingdom come.

Now I knew. I was about to drop a bombshell in own home.

It's blast range would be greater than I ever imagined. Cathy knew I was coming home that morning, but for her it was just another trip for me. Out to preach. Back in a couple days. It had happened hundreds of time over the course of our marriage.

Ron had arranged for our best friends, Doyle and Lucy Bishop to drive down from Tulsa to be there for Cathy and our boys. We climbed the sun-laden steps of our brand new model home we had purchased just months before. No words were said. I rang the door bell and we waited. The door finally opened and there was Cathy with a look of surprise, seeing Ron and our friends standing with me. Smiling curiously, she warmly exclaimed, "Hey Ron! Doyle and Lucy! What are you all doing here? Come on in!!"

Showing up with friends without warning was on the "no fly list" in our home. Like any wife, Cathy had to have some notice to make sure everything was tidy and in order. She later told me that at first, her knees went weak, thinking something terrible had happened to one of our boys. When that fear subsided, she surmised it must be April 1st—April Fools.

As I walked in the door, Cathy and I finally caught eyes and intuition told her it was about me. Something was very wrong. I dolefully asked her to retreat with me to our bedroom. Cautiously, she followed me in and sat down beside me at the end of our bed.

I had been a communicator all my life. I was good at it. But on this day, there were no right words. There was no good way to communicate that the life Cathy had known was now over. Somehow the ugly truth stumbled off my lips. To this day, I can't remember a word I said. All I know is that I made some feeble attempt to limit the shock and pain in my precious wife's life.

As if that were possible.

The sin and the secrets I had carefully concealed from Cathy for twenty-five years were finally laid bare. An absolute avalanche of sorrow, chased with pain, poured through her soul. She quickly stood up in her tears ... and confusion ... and then anger ... and little by little ... stepped backwards ... creating as much distance from me as she could.

Sobbing uncontrollably, she just looked at me. With shock and utter disgust. Nothing needed to be said. I felt every ounce of her pain. Her weeping was more devastating than words. She finally ran out of our bedroom into the arms of Ron and our friends. Huddled around her, all they could do was weep with her. There would be no cheering up. And everything wasn't going to be OK. The mood in our home turned as somber as a dirge.

My sin brought a great deal of pain to many people. None more than my family. And no one more than Cathy. The deception and betrayal she felt in that moment was indescribable. It would test every vow, every pledge, and every bond we had made in the course of our thirty year marriage.

The moment I thought this day couldn't get worse, we got the news that my youngest son Brock had been in a wreck and his car had been totaled. Thankfully he was not hurt, so I jumped in my truck to pick him up and bring him home, so I could meet with him, along with Jeremy and Dillon. It was the longest drive of my life. Brock's curiosity about our "family meeting" and my avoidance of any details was more than a little troublesome to him. But I just couldn't disclose something this traumatic during a car ride.

We finally pulled in the driveway and pushed the door open to see Jeremy and Dillon leering my direction with a look that can only be described as "what the hell have you done?" Only Cathy knew what I was about to say.

My boys were all their twenties now and they loved their father. They admired all that I had accomplished in life. On many levels, I had been a good and loving father. I spent time with them in their interests and hobbies. I prayed with them, walked them through their challenges growing up and I absolutely loved being their Dad. Every greeting and goodbye was accompanied by a kiss on the cheek. The Bartels were always a loving and affectionate crew.

I sat down on an ottoman, and I slowly waded through my

confession, finding it nearly impossible to make eye contact with anyone in this somber circle of family. Each admission that I spilled out was drenched in shame and met with shock. My tears seemed endless. I finally shut up. It was done.

Silence.

Seconds turned into minutes. Heads were dropped.

Until this.

My oldest son Jeremy, lifted his head. He looked at me. And he screamed, "F*CK! F*CK! F*CK!"

And he ran out our front door.

My heart instantly sunk. Oh my God. What have I done? Did I just lose my son forever? My mind transported me back to the first U2 concert I took Jeremy to. He was fifteen. There we were wringing wet in the power and emotion of our beloved band. As Bono began his thunderous call to take shelter from the poison rain—Jeremy and I embraced and wept together. In a moment, we were completely oblivious of 20,000 other human beings who had joined us at Reunion Arena in Dallas. It was a defining mo- ment in our pilgrimage together as Dad and son.

There was now a new moment. And it cast a pitch-black shad-ow on every iota of good I had done as his father.

As I leaned forward, covering my face with my hands, Brock walked over and put his hand on my shoulder, looking down at me and said, "Dad, just get yourself better." I've never seen him so solemn. He walked away.

In less than a few hundred seconds, the near perfect world of our lives and family collapsed in front of us. In the coming days, the pain and humiliation would only get worse as the Dallas

Morning News published a front page article about my scandal, with Christian publications and social media buzz and outrage to follow.

What I didn't tell you is how my middle son, Dillon reacted to my betrayal.

It would change my life forever.

Chapter Twenty

A GAY SON'S GRACE

I had greater dread about how Dillon would respond than the other two boys.

You see, just one year earlier, my worst fear came to pass. It turned out, the porn incident early on in Dillon's life wasn't just teenage curiosity. After graduating from high school, he confided in us that he was still struggling with strong impulses towards relationships with the same sex. I tried to tell him I understood what he was going through, but I really didn't. How could I? The idea of being with another man was repulsive to my very nature. And my highly charged Pentecostal upbringing told me that homosexuality was the basest of all sins. My "go-to" parental admonition went like this:

"Dillon, I understand it feels natural for you to be attracted to other men, but that doesn't make it right. Think about it like this … just because it feels natural for your Dad to be attracted to a woman other than your Mum, doesn't make it right for me to give into that temptation, does it?"

Yup. I said that. Looking back now, all I can say is, "Really Blaine? That's the best pile of horse shit you could come up with?"

Cathy and I asked Dillon to see a highly recommended family counselor in Dallas in hopes of finally finding the answers Dillon needed to walk out of this battle that had tormented him all of his adolescent years. Four months later, Dillon, who was now living in downtown Dallas with Jeremy, called us and said that he and his counselor wanted to meet with the two of us at his office.

Dillon seemed positive and upbeat, so we took that as a great sign. Perhaps finally he had conquered his demons!

A few days later, Cathy and I were sitting across from Dillon and his counselor. Dillon surveyed the room, and after a nod from the counselor, he began. He gently explained his desire to meet with us, "Mum and Dad, I want you know how much I love you and all that you have done to try to help me through the greatest challenge of my life." We continued to listen, now with a hint of uneasiness about what we were about to hear.

And then these words cut through the tension in the room, finding our unprepared ears …

"I have asked God every day to take these desires away from me. I tried to date girls and be attracted to them. I've gone to church and been on mission trips. And I've worked really hard with my counselor to become the person you want me to be. But in the end, I can't lie anymore. I am gay. As much as I've tried, I can't change myself into someone that I'm not. I am so sorry to disappoint you, but this is who I am."

The room was motionless. Shock. Dazed.

In a flash, rage filled every fiber of my being. How could he do this to us? Does he know how embarrassing this is going to be for me as a Pastor? How could he be so selfish and unthoughtful?

I blew up. Yelling and chastising, I told him he was foolish and heartless to put us though this. I warned that he would probably die an early death from aids or some other damnable ending of the life he was choosing. Our relationship was never the same after that. I hurt him in the worst way. What's sad, is I wanted to hurt him. Because he hurt me. When Dill needed the love of his father most, I abandoned him. I told him he was on his own from now on.

It was my worst day as a father.

Coming back to my confession, imagine the revelation of my rank duplicity registering on Dillon. It was as if I could hear his thoughts, "Wait a second Dad, you were doing all this bullshit while condemning me to hell for my sins?" My hypocrisy filled the room … and it was palpable.

And Dillon let me know in no uncertain terms how he felt about it.

He rose from the easy chair with tears coursing down his cheeks and didn't walk—he ran over to me—and kneeling at my feet, wrapped his arms around my legs, his voice trembling in the moment …

"Dad, I will never give up on you. I will never let you go. I love you so much. Please don't give up on yourself."

Author Cathleen Falsani wrote this …

"Justice is getting what you deserve. Mercy is not getting what you deserve. And grace is getting what you absolutely don't deserve … benign good will. Unprovoked compassion. The unearnable gift."

Dillon had just given his father the most incomprehensible gift of grace. He loved me in the most horrific moment of my life. And in that brief split second of time …

I encountered Jesus.

Chapter Twenty One

WHATCHA GONNA DO WHEN THEY COME FOR YOU

It was a beautiful spring day in Frisco, just warm enough to make life enjoyable, but without being overbearing or causing the day-long complaints that eventually come with the onset of summer.

In the midst of this beauty, down amongst the exhaust fumes and newly laid concrete of Legacy Drive—essentially a six-lane highway and one of the busiest streets in Frisco—I was out for a stroll. I stumbled along in mud-caked jeans, shuffling in a mostly straight line straight down the center of Legacy, distractedly sparking my BIC lighter with one hand while cupping my other hand around the cigarette dangling between my lips.

I wanted one last smoke before God took me, but the damn thing wouldn't light.

I took no notice of the abrasive honking, or the squealing rubber of suddenly averting tires as vehicles on this highly trafficked road swerved to avoid hitting me. I was too involved in that final cigarette to care about any of that.

Too focused on the ruins that were now caving in on my life. I wanted out of my world, and just like the blindfolded prisoners in classic films are given one final smoke before they face the firing squad, I felt entitled to this conclusive Marlboro Light.

Plus, if I was looking down at his lighter, I might not see the face of whatever unfortunate motorist wound up taking me out.

Just minutes before my ill-conceived stroll, I had looked into my parents' eyes and told them everything. It was the last of the face-to-face confessions I'd made that day about my double life.

My secret identity.

Blaine Bartel—that was my name in front of the curtains.
Ask anyone who knew me then and they'd tell you I was a great guy. As far as they knew, I was the "man of God" in my family, the voice that trumpeted the Good News of the gospel around the world, both in pulpits and on airwaves. He was the author of books, the host of national television shows, the always-humble rock star who rubbed shoulders with some of the biggest names in the Christian entertainment complex.

Curtis McKenzie—that was my back-stage name. That guy loved only himself. His eyes were glassy, intoxicated with pleasure. His voice gave only throaty howls of entitlement. His imagination knew no depth to its depravity, and it was a wellspring of death, incessantly gurgling forth new ideas to torture Blaine with. His mastery over Blaine seemed overwhelming, powered by the lethal, cold-blooded killer known as the god of gratification.

God had raised Blaine up.
And Curtis was bringing him down.

I'd just unleashed a torrent of torment in my parents' lives. While Cathy and the boys may have had their suspicions that something was awry in my world, Mum and Dad hadn't had a clue, and what I told them knocked their emotional breath out of them. I excused myself and headed to the backyard.

"I need a cigarette," I said.

I'd forgotten to tell them that I'd also taken up smoking. But that was the least of all our worries.

My house was only a mile or so away from my next destination, so I smoked that excuse-making cigarette, then carefully unlatched the gate in the back of my fence and started walking, making a more-or-less beeline to any oddly shaped building in the distance.

From a distance, it looked like a pile of boxes you might find on the floor of the closet in your spare room, but this was the home of Northstar Church, the brand-new building our four-year-old congregation had just moved into.

I purposefully walked through any mud I could find, conveniently located in a sort of drainage ditch that snaked through the tall, empty brown grass. My shoes sank deep into the filth, but I powered through it. I was working hard and getting soiled in the process.

I deserved it.

I wanted to get dirty. I was done with the clean-cut image—I wanted everyone to see who I really was. I wanted them to see Curtis.

I walked through the front doors of our handsome new church building, tracking in mud (and finally leaving a noticeable trace of my depravity) as I wandered the halls looking for our Assistant Pastor, Steven Pritt. I found him in his office.

"Steven," I said, "I need some church letterhead and an envelope." He looked me up and down with compassionate trepidation.

I'm sure he didn't know what to think of my mud-spewed pants and eyes red-rimmed from crying my soul out.

"Is everything okay, Pastor Blaine?" he said.

Yes: Pastor Blaine. The "Senior" part was unspoken but understood. I was the man in charge.

Not anymore.

"Yeah," I said, taking the paper from him. "I'll be back in a minute."

I made my way through the building we had opened just four months earlier, all the way to the back of the stage, where I sat on the floor and wrote my suicide note. I won't repeat it here, but the gist of it was apologizing and asking forgiveness from all the people I loved most in the world, including my wife Cathy; our three sons Jeremy, Dillon, and Brock; my parents and extended family; the staff at our church; and a few very close friends.

I sealed the letter in the envelope, the taste of envelope glue still finding its way to my tongue through cigarette residue and the saltiness of my tears. Then I got up and walked back to Steven's office.

"Give this to Ron Luce," I said, handing him the envelope. And without another word, I turned, walked out of that building forever, and out to meet my fate on Legacy Drive.

It was an aptly named street. The legacy I was leaving for my family, my friends, and all who knew me was this: I am a wreck and I don't deserve to live any longer. Might as well make it plain and leave my legacy on Legacy.

As the cars whisked by within inches of sending me to either hell or a hospital, I started making deals with God:

Take me now. For good.
Here's your chance.
Send a car.

End this miserable, painful existence.

Within a couple of minutes, God did send the perfect car. Five of them, in fact. Police cruisers. I was still trying to light that damn cigarette.

The wonderful men and women of Frisco law enforcement surrounded me, guns drawn, and began barking orders at me.

"Put your hands on your head and get down!"
"Get down now!"
"We will shoot! Get down!"

I was in a daze, but I figured out how to comply with their wishes. I dropped my lighter, let the cigarette fall from my lips, put my hands on the back of my head, and lowered myself until my knees felt the abrupt, pockmarked surface of the concrete street.

"Lie down!" they commanded.

I did, the discomforting grit of the concrete digging into my cheek as an officer put his knee in my back just before swinging my arms behind me to cuff them at the wrists. Now I had actual shackles pressing into me, binding me, holding me back. Fitting.

One of the officers got me upright and walked me over to a squad car, gently propping me in a sitting position against the front tire.

"What the hell are you doing?" he exclaimed.

I have no recollection of what I told him. I only know I mumbled and babbled like a crazy man.

"Who are you?" he asked. "What do you do? Where do you work?"

"I'm the pastor of that church," I said, nodding my head in the direction of the jumbled-boxes building with the slanted walls. "Northstar Church."

Oh, those walls. They were the talk of Frisco—why did they make those walls slanted? Perhaps it's because the pastor was off-center with his warped mind.

The officer just stared at me, trying to get a bead on how sober I was, I guess. Then he narrowed his eyes. "Problems at home?"

My eyes were out of tears by now—I'd cried them all out over the past few hours—but they must've looked honest and sad, because I somehow managed to convince these officers to take me back home instead of to the psych ward of a hospital.

Cathy, the boys, and my parents were searching for me outside the front door of our home when the police cruiser pulled into the driveway and spat me out of the back door like Jonah.

Before I could go in, the officers had to follow protocol by removing any guns from the house and requesting—demanding, really—a 24-hour watch on my life. My family agreed and off the police went, leaving me somehow even more humiliated than I already was.

It was an extremely uncomfortable, though uneventful night. I was locked in my bedroom while my family made phone call after phone call and, after cashing in a few favors, secured my next place to live.

And the irony of my future home was not lost on anyone.

Chapter Twenty Two
AMERICA'S POSTER CHILD

The following day I got off a plane in Phoenix, Arizona and was immediately spirited to Psychological Counseling Services—or PCS—one of the premier treatment centers in America for those who suffer from sexual addiction (or make others suffer from it).

America's place for perverts, I thought.
And that was me.

But first it was off to my living quarters for the next month. The Dream Center. This converted hotel was an outreach of Pastor Tommy Barnett of Phoenix First Assembly. It housed men and women that were brought in off the streets, mostly drug and alcohol addicts. I had taken a team of young people to Pastor Barnett's Dream Center several years earlier to minister to the "down and out." Well guess who was down and out now?

I was hauled back and forth to PCS from the Dream Center by a young "pastor in training" who was an unstoppable, and at times, annoying force for Jesus. First, he would not stop calling me "Pastor Blaine." I kept telling him, "Bro, I'm not a pastor anymore. Just call me Blaine."

He would just look over at me in his older, but immaculately kept car and smile, "Oh no Pastor Blaine. God's call will never leave you. You are a mighty man of God!!" As long as I live, I will never forgets this young man's words or his compassion. Even if I thought he was crazy at the time.

Shortly after checking in my suitcase at the Dream Center, I was dropped off at the home of Dr. Ralph Earle, the founder of PCS. I was escorted into his personal office. The walls were lined with books that had intimidating titles and the soft hum of the cooling fan of his computer was the only sound as I sat there and waited for help.

I needed this guy to fix me. Instead, he fixed his eyes on mine and with a deep, calming voice, said, "Blaine, tell me your story."

My story? This wasn't a nursery rhyme. This wasn't something you share with the kiddos before bed. This was twenty years of heart-wrenching, life-stealing, marriage-drowning, shame-manu-facturing misery.

This wasn't a story—this was me.

Year by year, one scandalous episode after another, I chronicled my deadly descent into the deep, dark hole of my enslavement to lust. It was the first time in twenty years that I had told anyone …

Everything.

Once again, the non-stop ocean of tears were streaming down my eyes. The ugly twins of shame and disgrace were sitting on my shoulders, whispering into each ear, "You are the most deplorable human being on the earth." And I believed them.

Telling my story felt more like reading my own obituary, be-cause the time had come for me to pay for all of my sins. And I knew the wages would demand death.

Death to my family.
Death to my soul … well, that had come a long time ago.

When I had finally chronicled my humiliating litany of decadence, Dr. Earle gathered has breath, leaned forward and looked deep into my glazed over eyes and uttered words I will never forget.

"Blaine, right now you are the poster child for sexual addiction in America."

It was a moment of crystal-like clarity.

There was nothing Dr. Earle hadn't seen. Nothing he hadn't heard. He had treated rock stars, Hollywood celebrities, professional athletes and millionaire moguls … all the people America has come to expect this kind of out-of-control behavior from.

I was none of these. But I had made it to the top of his crazy list. He wasn't finished.

His next words were, "Blaine, you can't even begin to fathom the work you are going to have to do to find freedom." And then he uttered the words that would eventually become my call to arms, "I honestly don't know if you are going to make it. We will see."

Welcome to my beautiful battle. My fantastic fight. My wonderful war. My bewitching brawl.

It was a fight for the beauty of hope.
It was a fight for the beauty of relationships.
It was a fight for the beauty of freedom.
It was a fight for the beauty of grace …
… and for a thing called resurrection.

Scene Three

RESURRECTION

"As soon as the generals and the politicos can predict the motions of your mind, lose it. Leave it as a sign to mark the false trail, the way you didn't go. Be like the fox who makes more tracks than necessary, some in the wrong direction. Practice resurrection."

—Wendell Berry

Chapter Twenty Three

DOING THE DIRTY WORK

You have patiently waded through my best attempt to honestly tell the story of my spiral into death.

In the closing chapters, you are going to bear witness to my life plot taking a dramatic twist that I assure you I never saw coming. From the second I landed at Psychological Counseling Services in Phoenix and forward through the literal thousands of hours of counseling I received, there was one dominant word communicated to me again and again:

Recovery.

The goal was to get back my life. To fully recover all that I had lost to my sin and addiction. And then about two years into my recovery, I was driving from Kansas City to Tulsa praying. Not an out-loud, petitioning kind of prayer. More of an introspective listening kind of prayer. I heard the whisper of the Spirit in my soul, "Blaine, I'm not offering you recovery. I am calling out your resurrection."

That word from heaven changed everything in my journey back. I began to see there was really nothing in my old life that I truly wanted to recover. My old way of thinking … my old way of relating to others, my old way of encountering God … it all needed to be left dead and buried. Jesus was resurrecting a way of living that I had never imagined before.

Would I see it? Would I have the courage to take it? I was drawn to the story of Lazarus in the gospel of John. I began reading in verse one of chapter eleven.

"A man was sick, Lazarus of Bethany, the town of Mary and her sister Martha. This was the same Mary who massaged the Lord's feet with aromatic oils and then wiped them with her hair. It was her brother Lazarus who was sick. So the sisters sent word to Jesus, "Master, the one you love so very much is sick." When Jesus got the message, he said, "This sickness is not fatal. It will become an occasion to show God's glory by glorifying God's Son."

Hmm … my eyes gazed down to verse thirty-three …

"When Jesus saw her sobbing and the Jews with her sobbing, a deep anger welled up within him. He said, 'Where did you put him?' 'Master, come and see,' they said. Now Jesus wept. The Jews said, 'Look how deeply he loved him.' Others among them said, 'Well, if he loved him so much, why didn't he do something to keep him from dying? After all, he opened the eyes of a blind man.'"

I read on, more and more intrigued by the mounting tension in the story between Jesus and the family.

"Then Jesus, the anger again welling up within him, arrived at the tomb. It was a simple cave in the hillside with a slab of stone laid against it. Jesus said, 'Remove the stone.' The sister of the dead man, Martha, said, 'Master, by this time there's a stench. He's been dead four days!' Jesus looked her in the eye. 'Didn't I tell you that if you believed, you would see the glory of God?'"

I knew what was next, but the text still washed over me like a wave in the ocean tide.

"Then, to the others, 'Go ahead, take away the stone.'
They removed the stone. Jesus raised his eyes to heaven
and prayed, 'Father, I'm grateful that you have listened to
me. I know you always do listen, but on account of this
crowd standing here I've spoken so that they might believe that you sent me.' Then he shouted, 'Lazarus, come
out!' And he came out, a cadaver, wrapped from head
to toe, and with a kerchief over his face. Jesus told them,
'Unwrap him and let him loose.'"

John 11:1-4; 17-44 The Message

Resurrection is a dirty thing. There is the sobbing.

A foul smell of life decomposing.
The prying of death out of the earth.
Rags filthy and stained.
A man standing naked before the world.

Just when everyone thought it was over.

Life.

But don't believe for one damn minute that the marvel of resur-
rection is easy. The death of days between Good Friday and Easter
Sunday can be horrific at times. But it is a miraculous journey that
I would never take back.

The path of resurrection is worth every breath of our
broken existence.

George Whitefield was one the great preachers of the 18th century who helped to inspire the Methodist movement. He said this
about resurrection:

"The sinner can no more raise himself from the deadness of sin than Lazarus, who had been dead four days, until Jesus came."

Coming out of my sin demanded resurrection, not rehab.

In the years ahead, as I navigated through attempts to save my marriage, regain a relationship with my sons, rediscover family and friendship, reimagine my life's work, the Lord graciously unearthed seven dirty little secrets of resurrection in my life.

The truths He revealed and then taught me to practice completely transformed the way I approach and live life today. Jesus called my name as I lay dead in that dark, spartan room at the Dream Center and said, "Come forth."

The progress of technology nor the passage of time has changed the capacity of Christ to transform lives. As He said to the dead and dirty Lazarus, so Jesus calls to you and me: "Come forth."

Come forth from the chains of sin.
Come forth from the despair of depression.
Come forth from the death of ourselves.
Come forth to a life you've never dared to imagine.
Come forth.

Chapter Twenty Four

RESURRECTIONS ARE
ALWAYS TOO LATE

When I boarded my flight from Phoenix back to Tulsa after a full month of rehab, I honestly did not feel any more free from my addictive behavior than the day I entered.

I had completely dedicated myself to everything I was asked to do. Twelve hours day. Six days a week. For an entire month. The combined counseling hours I received in one month was equal to going to a counselor once a month for five years. It was beyond intense.

Group therapy. (oh, I'm not the only schmuck puppet)
Role play therapy. (drama class for addicts)
Equine therapy. (Hey, who doesn't love horses?)
Guided therapeutic imagery. (don't ask)
Childhood trauma work. (very unpleasant crap)
Art therapy. (drawing strange things)
Psychodrama therapy. (Breaking Bad in rehab)

Some of it was weird, but I didn't care. I was desperate and everything I had tried to cure myself hadn't worked. So bring on a stampede of wild horses, if that's what's needed.

Without question, the most grueling time in rehab was the two weeks Cathy came in to join me. I had to do what they called "full disclosure" of my awful secret life. There is some debate in the recovery world as to whether disclosing all of an addict's arcane behavior to a spouse is really healthy for the future of a marriage. But the therapists at PCS believed it was absolutely necessary and Cathy absolutely wanted to know everything. And if our roles were reversed, I would have expected the same—nothing less than the entire truth of what happened, no matter how ugly.

It took two full days to complete my disclosure to Cathy with our counselors guiding us. She literally passed out twice due to the sheer shock and trauma. With each revelation of my past, I saw her spirit breaking more and more. By the time it was over, I felt like I had utterly destroyed her with the repugnant realities of my past. Her pain and tears were unbearable at times.

But I forced myself to take her pain in.
I made myself feel it.
I needed it.
It made me begin to feel human again.

Before going to PCS, Cathy had given me every indication that she was committed to saving our marriage. I honestly had no doubts she would work through this with me. She has always been the most loving and caring soul. However, when we left, things had changed. She had all the sordid details now. And with each revelation, the pain mounted in her soul. This wouldn't be as easy to overcome as we both thought it would be. Cathy and I briefly separated after PCS to contemplate the possibility of a future together.

While I was at PCS, more than one thousand people trekked through the doors to the first Easter Sunday ever in our brand new building at Northstar Church. To their surprise, their Pastor would not be there on the biggest Sunday in the history of our church. Rather Ron Luce would read my resignation message.

The room was filled with shock and within days, shock spun

into anger, as bits and pieces of my story began to circulate through the congregation. And I understood every bit of their ire. I had let them down in the worst way.

A few days later, a reporter for the Dallas Morning News called me, requesting an interview. His article was published a day later with the headline:

"PASTOR OF FRISCO'S NORTHSTAR CHURCH QUITS OVER INFIDELITY."

I would find out later that when my oldest son went to work the next day, some of his co-workers had seen the paper and curiously began to question him about what had happened. For the first time in his life, Jeremy was embarrassed to say that I was his father.

The last paragraph of that reporter's article went like this:

Steven Pritt, Northstar's assistant pastor, released a statement … "Our prayers are with Blaine Bartel and his family," Pritt said.

Whatever prayers were being prayed didn't seem to be working. At least that's what it felt like. Our family was in complete chaos. The damage I had caused was catastrophic. And as I looked back at all my choices … all my sin … the scorched trail of destruction that the fires of my lust had left for all of us to try to pilot through—it was all insufferable.

My head was constantly riddled with the "whys" in my daily struggle to try to pick my family off the ground. Why didn't I come clean early on in my life? Why did I think hiding my sin would be better for my family?

Why??????

As I scrutinized the narrative of Lazarus, the same questions were asked of Jesus. Why didn't he get here when Lazarus was alive and there was still a chance. I'm sure there were thoughts in the crowd around the tomb as Jesus arrived four days late, "Way to go Jesus. You're a little late now man. Sheesh!!"

I had to come to a place in my life where I ripped off the rear view mirror and stopped asking the "why" questions. Because the very nature of resurrection is this:

Resurrections are always too late.
There has never been an on time resurrection. Ever.
Someone died. Something had to end.

I really don't think Lazarus spent the rest of his life regretting the days he spent dead in a cold grave. He was celebrating a life he couldn't have possibly imagined without Jesus. When Jesus calls us forth from the "death space" in our lives, we can't look back.

Eyes forward and press the accelerator down. Life is about to get better. Way better.

We all have things in our life that need to die and be buried.

Ego and pride.
Sin and strongholds. Hurt and unforgiveness.
Faithlessness and failure.

The list goes on and on. The first step in experiencing the glory of resurrection is to be willing to let whatever needs to die in our life … be buried. Let the death in your life—die. Once and for all. It's not resuscitation, it's resurrection.

Stop the speculation of how things might have been.

Chapter Twenty Five
RESURRECTIONS STINK
BEFORE THEY START

Before Jesus called Lazarus out of the grave, his sister Martha warned Jesus, "Lord, by this time he stinks!"

Pre-resurrection stinks. And my life was in pre-resurrection mode.

My addiction stunk.
My marriage stunk.
My religion stunk.
My ministry career was also officially in the crapper.

Now back in Dallas, it was time to begin the hard work of picking up the pieces of our lives and trying to rebuild. My computer and cell phones were disposed of, along with all my social media and email accounts. The past had to be completely erased, disconnecting me from any chance of putting defibrillators on Curtis McKenzie.

There was some part of me that was relieved to be completely out of ministry. When I told Ron Luce that I wanted to resign, he talked about putting together a "restoration team" for me. I asked him what kind restoration he was talking about. He replied

"Restoration of your spiritual health and ministry." My immediate response was, "Forget ministry. That's over for me."

You see, I wanted a chance to rediscover God without the trappings and strings that are attached with the professional obligations of ministry. I had come to a place in my life where I had more questions about God than answers. I resented most of what I saw on Christian television and yet, these were the very ministers that I was rubbing shoulders with. I was bewildered by preachers that were downright gleeful when they talked about people who didn't measure up to their moral yardstick, telling them they were going to hell. And frankly, I questioned my own faith.

After all, if the power of the Holy Spirit was really all I believed it was, why wasn't it formidable enough to give me the strength to stop my own insane behavior?

So I resolved to become a spiritual free agent.

I wasn't turning my back on God, but I was wise enough to know that my faith in days gone by had failed me profoundly. Please understand I don't believe God failed me. And I don't believe the church failed me. I believe what I believed about God and the church failed me. So I prayed a very sincere prayer, "God—whoever you are, I am asking you to reveal yourself to me."

I began reading books about God and religion that I had never dared to read. I opened up my heart to other religious streams of thought. Because my faith was no longer tied to my income, I was free for the first time in my life to have an intellectually honest deliberation and quest for truth.

I can tell you today that in no uncertain terms, Jesus revealed himself to me in a way I have never experienced before. Not the charismatic circus show Jesus. Not the white evangelical Jesus. Not the fundamental rule-keeping Jesus. And not the American flag-waving, political Jesus.

The resurrected Jesus.
The Jesus of the early church.
The Jesus that threw parties for prodigals.
The Jesus that ripped on religion.
The Jesus that laughed at the impossible.

I came to a complete place of humility and recognition of how much the filth of my sin and religious pride stunk in the very nostrils of God. I leaned into the Psalms. They brought language to what I was feeling.

"My wounds stink, they are corrupt, because of my foolishness. I am depressed; I am bowed down beyond measure; I go mourning all the day."

Psalm 38:5-6 (Darby Translation)

Growing up skiing, I stood at the top of the highest mountains in North America. The views were amazing. It is the closest thing to seeing through the eyes of God.

There are two 'mountain stories" in scripture that thoroughly changed my view of God.

Moses climbed a mountain to receive the ten commandments. He climbed alone. He came down with rules. And the people failed at checking all the boxes. We all failed. That was the purpose of the law. It was a school teacher. Paul told the Galatians "...the law was our schoolmaster to bring us unto Christ, that we might be justified by faith." (Galatians 3:24)

Jesus on the other hand, invited his disciples to climb a mountain with him. They climbed together. And they didn't come down with rules. They descended with a revelation. The mount of transfiguration is the ultimate revelation of who God is ... at least for me. When Jesus goes to the top of a mountain with Peter, James and John, something amazing happens. Transfigured before them is Moses (the Law), Elijah (the Prophets) and of course Jesus. (the Son of God)

Suddenly, Moses and Elijah disappear and only Jesus is left. Then the Father speaks from the heavens. "This is my beloved Son, listen to Him."

Do we see it?

Jesus completely eclipsed the law and the prophets.

Jesus is the exact representation of God. He alone is who we listen to. Everything that came before Him, fell short of showing us what God was really like. The law fell short. The prophets fell short. Their only job was to expose our utter need for the Son.

We don't find our freedom or faith in the Old Testament. God isn't speaking to us anymore through the law and the prophets. They had their purpose in pointing us to the Son, but they should disappear from our gaze to know God. Jesus is enough. Jesus is all. Listen to Him. He is what God looks like. He is what God acts like. He is what God has to say. I must thank Pastor Brian Zahnd more than anyone else for helping me to understand this.

Being out of ministry and unable to find a decent paying job began to cripple us financially. Our savings were disappearing faster than a rabbit in David Copperfield's hat. The board of Trustees paid us two months severance after my resignation. I remember being so mad at Ron (Luce) about this, that I hung up the phone on him. We had given our lives to building this church. We had helped countless others in their moments of crisis. But when our crisis came, I felt abandoned. (To Ron's great credit, he would personally raise money to help us through several months)

The financial need was more about my family than it was me. Cathy and our children were the innocents in all of this and I felt like they were being forgotten in the wake of my sin. Ron and our board of trustees invited Pastor Robert Morris and Gateway Church to help navigate our congregation in their search for a new pastor. Within a few months, the decision was made to give the church to Pastor Morris and Gateway, and it was cannibalized into one of their extension campuses.

I was both happy and crestfallen at the same time. I was happy that Gateway Church was helping in so many ways to save the day for Northstar Church. They provided strong and loving leadership to our suffering community and sustained the church financially through all the upheaval. Yet I was bitterly disappointed that our family felt very little support from Pastor Morris or his key pastors. While graciously saving our church community, I felt like they failed to love a broken pastor's family in the process.

No one came to our home. There was no phone call asking how we were doing. We were told not to return to our church and our church community was told not to contact us. I don't share this to blame anyone. It was just our reality at the time. Navigating the moral failure of a pastor is complicated to say the least. In the end, I sinned. And the fallout started and ended with me.

Regretfully, I wrote Pastor Morris a very nasty email during this trying season, detailing my disappointment in their lack of care for our family. I never received a response. (and I understand why) But two years later, I sat across the table from him. I will share that conversation a little later.

Meanwhile, Cathy and I spent the next year trying to figure out if our marriage was repairable. Scripturally she had every right to leave me. I was unfaithful and an adulterer. And coming home from the full disclosure of my twenty-plus year history of sexual sin, she was experiencing the fresh wounds of both betrayal and rejection.

Each week, we gathered ourselves and took our old pains and new problems to our counselor, Dr. Ken McGill. Dr. McGill is a giant of a man and an ordained pastor. He stands over six foot and you wouldn't want to get in his way on a football field. But when I say "giant" it is much more in terms of his huge heart for people. Ken is in his fifties and before starting his private practice in Dallas, was personally mentored by Dr. Patrick Carnes, a pioneer in the field of sex addiction work. He is also the former Director of the Gentle Path Program in Mississippi. (this is where Tiger Woods went after his admission to his numerous affairs) Needless to say, we had the best counselor we could possibly hope for to guide us out of our mayhem.

Another important detail about Dr. Ken. He had recently lost his thirteen year old daughter, Marissa, to an awful car accident. When I think about the inconceivable grief he pushed through in his own life, to so carefully carry us through our pain, I can only look back in awe. He is one of the heroes in our family.

Our sessions were grueling. It was one yard forward and a cloud of dust each time. And then on the tense drive home, I often felt like we would lose whatever ground we had gained as we attempted to process what we had discussed in the disarray of our strange new lives. We would walk into our empty house (our boys were now living together downtown) and Cathy would go to her bedroom and I would go to my new living quarters upstairs.

Every couple months, I would ask Cathy, "Are you ready to commit to go forward in our marriage?" Her response always indicated a desire to commit, but seemed unable to break through the continuing pain and ugly imaginations of my betraying past. I think I pushed her too hard to try to heal too quickly. I know it frustrated her when I would continually ask if she was "doing any better."

I've learned you can't put a timeline on healing a broken heart. Nor can new trust be supernaturally conjured up. Every person heals differently. Cathy had forgiven me. But there is a colossal difference between forgiveness and re-entering a relationship that risks encountering the same pain all over again.

Making things even worse was that all of this happened during the economic crash of 2009-2010. Most of the money we had saved over the years was put into our house as equity. When the market went upside down, we lost it all when we couldn't keep up with the bank payments and eventually our house went into foreclosure. When it rains, it pours. In our case, when it rains, get ready because a hurricane is on the way.

Death stinks. Our decaying and degenerating existence had a certain stench to it. People were avoiding me. Friends had dropped off. How could I blame them? I didn't even like be- ing around myself. And sometimes, it feels like the stink never ends. As if our life is one endless garbage dump and no matter where we go, we cannot escape it's foul odor.

Yet.

Jesus was not afraid of Lazarus's stink, and he's not afraid of ours. He just rolls away the stone of our foul, reeking tomb and calls for the life of God to resurrect our aching soul.

Sin is foul. It is humiliating and scandalous. But it is precisely why Jesus stepped into death on Good Friday and burst back to life on Easter Sunday!

The first year post-crisis was hard. Harder than I could have imagined. There were times I wanted to give up on life. Times that I wanted to just run headlong into the world and taste all that it had to offer.

I was ready for a sign ... any sign ... of resurrection in my life. But there was one more death I had to encounter.

Chapter Twenty Six
WHEN OTHERS CALL YOU DEAD, JESUS CALLS YOUR NAME

If there is one thing I have discovered looking back at my crash, it is this … we never sin unto ourselves.

When our lies and betrayal come out, it has a ripple effect on so many other lives. And for many, it is much more than a ripple. It is a tsunami.

The one person who felt the greatest ache of the soul was my precious wife Cathy. I don't know of another person in this world who has more compassion and sincerity than her. There was nothing she wouldn't do for someone in need and was beloved by our church family at Northstar. She resisted public ministry, rather was happy to love and pray for people in more private settings.

She was also a peerless Mum. She threw herself into raising our boys, often without a lot of help from me because of my unabating travel schedule. Every birthday and holiday was special—because Cathy made it special.

The best way to describe our marriage prior to my confession was a really close friendship. Any real intimacy had vacated our relationship many years before. You can hold me responsible for that. With all the porn and fantasy in my secret world, the real work of keeping the romantic fires burning had become uninteresting to me. Frankly put, porn sets up any marriage for failure. There is a better chance of Hillary Clinton paying for a night at a Trump hotel than a wife being able to compete with porn actors being paid to perform their absurd charades.

In spite of our lack of intimacy, we both cared deeply for each other. Cathy had weathered the gut-wrenching early deaths of both her Mum and Dad and I had done my best to love her through those terrible losses. I was also very close with Cathy's brother David and sister Joanne. I suppose on some level I had become a surrogate father to both of them.

But in the end, despite all of our counseling and Cathy's courageous efforts to restore our marriage, we failed.

I'm going to let that sit there for a minute.

Here's why. Our divorce would be without question the worst of all the repercussions of my sin. It was more than heart-wrenching. It sucks the very life force out of your soul. Our parting was never hostile. Cathy simply could not get beyond the overpowering sense of betrayal and the deep wounds that I had inflicted on her heart.

There was no ugly court battle. We met with an attorney together that our counselor had recommended. I asked what the maximum spousal maintenance a Texas court could award. The lawyer wrote down the monthly amount and number of years on a yellow legal pad, pushed it over to me and I asked to pay it. I honestly wish I could have done even more. There have been years since our divorce that I have paid more in alimony than I have made in salary. I just found a way to keep it up. Cathy had given her life to me. And I had failed her. She deserved better.

Even after our divorce, there was a season of time that we both had hoped for some sort of "fairy tale" reconciliation. A year and half later, I actually moved back to Dallas for one month to see if we could possibly make it work again. This time, I was the one that couldn't get there. As much as I tried, I felt helpless in rekindling a new and healthy relationship. I don't know if too much time had passed or if it was this nagging fear that wouldn't go away—that I would fail again and hurt Cathy even more.

Today, Cathy is one of the heroes in my story. It has taken her a good measure of time, prayer and the grace of Jesus in her life, but I know she has completely forgiven me and remains my very good friend. More than a friend, really. It's hard to explain. We shared thirty years of life together. We parented three amazing boys who have now grown into accomplished young men. Together, we are still Mum and Dad to our sons and we share that privilege with joy. I pray for Cathy often. And I know she prays for me.

In the years that followed our divorce, I went through seasons of lostness, amplified by intense loneliness. It was disorienting being single for the first time in thirty years. I was also coping with the stigma of being a divorced minister. I remember the first time I saw an old friend from my ministry world who hadn't got wind of my crisis. He innocently asked, "What's Cathy up to today?" I stumbled for an answer. I did my best to give a snapshot explanation of why we were no longer married, standing with my grocery cart at the front door of Target. After listening to my rambling debacle, there was a change in his tone and said he would pray for me, as he made a beeline for his car.

Some of my closest friends stopped taking my calls. In fact, one of my best friends told me, "Blaine, I really can't hang out with you anymore. My wife just doesn't want you around anymore." For the first time in my life, I was experiencing the pain of rejection.

God, it hurt.

Then there were the stories of my name being dragged through the evangelical world's mud by former preacher friends. I had

137

become the topic of many a blog, social media post, as well as a cautionary story in pulpits.

The wounds were going deeper than I anticipated. I have never paid much attention to what other people thought about me. Well that's easy when you're riding a wave of success everyday. Criticism during times of triumph and affluence are like nerf bullets. But when you're already broken and humiliated, each incrimination, however true it may be, is like a poisonous arrow to the heart.

There was a certain empathy I began to feel for the lepers I read about in scripture. Untouchable. Discarded. Even though I knew I had brought every bit of this on myself, I felt powerless in stopping the bitterness from seeping into my soul. It was during this time that God brought some people into my life that I never counted on.

Michael Caney and his wife Becca were two friends from our church that wouldn't let me go. I hardly knew them before my fall into grace, (not from grace) but they were determined to see me through my calamity, knowing all along I had brought it on myself. They loved me through all of my folly, pride and heartbreak. One afternoon, as Michael and I sat, watching a conveyer belt of rainbow rolls and sashimi parade by at our favorite lunch haunt, I turned to him and said, "Bro, it's over. I kind of think the church is done with me. And honestly, I think I'm done with the church."

He gently put his hand on my shoulder and said words that have never left me, "Blaine, Jesus is destroying your kingdom and he is building His kingdom in your life. And wherever you run, he will be there waiting for you. You aren't going anywhere."

Then there was one of the many tennis games with my friend Kevin Cortez. Kevin was a leader in our church who was a former pastor and became a trusted confidante in my attempts to rebuild my life. Tennis with him was therapeutic. I remember him being ahead of me 5-0 in one game. One more game and the set was his.

Normally, I would throw away the last game and live for another day. Not today. I dug deep and was determined to bid for a comeback. I ended up winning 7-5. Kevin walked over at the end of our match and asserted, "Blaine, you're a champion. Any time you feel any different, remember this day. Comebacks are in your blood."

What a friend he has been.

Not long after that day, I received a Facebook message from a woman from Canada. Her name was Carla and though I did not know her, she asked me to pray for a mutual friend that I had competed with in freestyle skiing years ago. As we corresponded, she had such a beautiful way of communicating the love of Jesus. She was also very attractive. I found out later she had dated Wayne Gretzky years before, which only heightened my curiosity about her. I was scheduled to be in Canada in about eight weeks and we decided to meet up while I was there.

We absolutely hit it off. The emptiness and loneliness I was experiencing in this season of my life was quenched by her vibrant heart. She shared a compassion for me and all that I had been through, even if I thought I didn't deserve it. She was extremely intelligent and well-educated theologically. Carla had also been through an addiction recovery training program and had a passion to help others walk in the freedom of Christ. We met every day I was in Canada and each time she would share new insights into the grace of God and the sheer joy of living in freedom.

I had never met anyone quite like her. Although we both committed to keep our relationship free of any sexual encumbrance, we both had developed an earnest romantic attraction. In the end, it only lasted for a few months, mainly because we lived a couple thousand miles apart. And perhaps even more, because I don't feel we were ever meant to be a couple, as much as we were meant to be friends during this time. The things she taught me about Jesus and the goodness of God transformed the way I live today.

As I was flying home after a trip to Canada, she urged, "Blaine, when you get home, just sit in the solitude of your living room. Invite Jesus to sit with you. And rest in the moment." Weird right? So with a mix of skepticism and holy intrigue, I walked through the door of my eighteenth floor apartment, left my luggage at the door and with measured intention, walked over to my couch. I sat down. I took a deep breath and slowly exhaled ...

"Jesus, I invite you to sit down with me."

My eyes were closed. Not tightly. More like a peaceful shutting out of the world around me. And I just waited silently. A presence filled the room. I felt someone walking across the room. Sensing the weight of someone sitting down beside me, I heard a voice that can only be described as the deepest reverberation of kindness. I felt a strong hand clasp my shoulder, and these words followed, "Blaine, I'm here. I love you."

In the midst of all my aloneness, Jesus was present. He called my name.

Did you see Him Blaine? I did. In friends like Michael, Kevin and Carla. When others were calling me dead and used up, they called me forth.

I was the second-chance Jonah.
I was the newly strengthened Samson.
I was the freshly inaugurated Peter.
I was the paradise-promised thief on the cross.

When I was at my gutter-bound lowest, Jesus was there. Years ago, I had the privilege of meeting one of my favorite authors, Max Lucado. In one of his books, he wrote ...

"Does God care if I'm sad? Look at the tear-streaked face of Jesus as He stands near Lazarus's tomb."

Jesus weeps over our brokenness. When others are calling for our head, He is calling our name.

Death is over-rated. Resurrection trumps the cold, damp shadows of death's dark valley—every time. Listen for your name. He's calling you. And He's using beautiful human beings that you least expected to show up in your zero-hour.

Chapter Twenty Seven
THE GRAVE CLOTHES MUST COME OFF

Immediately after Jesus called Lazarus out of the grave, out walked an undead man.

Fully alive. But fully covered in rags of death.

Jesus told Lazarus's family and friends to "Unwrap him and let him loose." Mary, Martha, family and friends who were gathered to say goodbye, were now unexpectedly given the task of unraveling the grave clothes of Lazarus from head to foot.

And there Lazarus stood. Naked before the world.

One of the most important parts of my resurrection undertaking was allowing the Spirit to help me find the humility to let the people I loved and trusted into my story. In sharing my secrets, my struggles and my story, there was hope and healing.

Allow me for a moment to speak candidly about "restoring ministers." There is so much misinformation about how we are to restore those who have experienced moral failure while in ministry. One of the first things that Ron Luce put into place in my life was a "restoration team" of three men who were responsible for my spiritual recovery. One was Ken Blount, a friend who I had served alongside for years at *Church on the Move* in Tulsa. Some of you may know him as Nicodemus from the Gospel Bill Show.

Pastor Roy Evans was also on my team. Roy is a good friend and the former camp director for Church on the Move's camp, Dry Gulch USA. Lastly, there was one of my best friends, Doyle Bishop who is a local Tulsa businessman.

Let me tell you how this worked. It didn't.

Each of these men did their best to lob the occasional phone call and see how I was doing. I have no doubt they loved me and did everything they could to help, but ultimately each of them were too busy in their own lives to be worried about mine. What they provided for me was love and support. And I remain grateful to this very day for every effort they made to help me and my family.

But here's the bottom line. If I really wanted restoration, it was wasn't up to some team to provide it for me. I had to be hungry enough to want it and be relentless in finding resurrection in my life.

Restoration teams don't fail. Those seeking restoration fail to want it enough.

I made a commitment to find the people in my life to help take off my old graves clothes. The early church leader, Paul, put it like this to the believers in Rome …

"The night is almost gone; the day of salvation will soon be here. So remove your dark deeds like dirty clothes, and put on the shining armor of right living. Because we belong to the day, we must live decent lives for all to see. Don't participate in the darkness of wild parties and drunkenness, or in sexual promiscuity and immoral living, or in quarreling and jealousy. Instead, clothe yourself with the presence of the Lord Jesus Christ. And don't let yourself think about ways to indulge your evil desires."

Romans 13:12-14 New Living Translation

I began opening my heart up to other men in three different men's groups every week. I engaged weekly with a couple of really close friends in Dallas, sharing my victories and defeats along the way. I leaned in deeply to my immediate family, asking them to help me see my blind spots on the road to resurrection. I would not be here today without my Mum and Dad. My Mum sent me a text message every single day in the first two years of my recovery with a word of strength and truth. My sister Luanne, my brother Jason and their beautiful families were there for me as well.

But I couldn't wait for any of these friends and family to come and pick me up every time I stumbled. I had to continually reach out for help. I went to church every time the doors were open.

One church I found great solace in was Watermark Church and Pastor Todd Wagner. They welcomed me with so much mercy and love and their pastors reached out to me in a way that surprised me, being a mega-church in the city. I engaged in their Friday night addiction recovery program and it brought new levels of health into my life.

Of course, Ron Luce was with me every step of the way. And the greatest thing about Ron's guidance through my restoration back to life, is that the process was never punitive, but always redemptive. There was never a feeling that I was being punished for screwing up, but being given time to fully heal. The idea that ministers should be put in the "penalty box" for two or three years to learn their lesson is foolish and shaming. The reason a pastor needs time away from ministry is to allow their soul to heal and to learn how to be transformed in their thinking and behavior. And that all takes time.

It took me three years before I would be in a place to re-engage in public ministry, though I stayed involved in local churches helping and volunteering behind the scenes. If you are a minister who has been overcome by immorality, please love yourself and your family enough to step away from the grind for the time needed to be whole. We all know it takes grace to step on the stage—but I believe it takes an even greater grace to step off.

I love how the Apostle Paul described our response to those who have been caught in sin …

> "Brothers, if anyone is caught in any sin, you who are spiritual [that is, you who are responsive to the guidance of the Spirit] are to restore such a person in a spirit of gentleness [not with a sense of superiority or self-righteousness], keeping a watchful eye on yourself, so that you are not tempted as well."

Galations 6:1 Amplified Translation

The text here implores us to restore such a one with a gentle spirit, void of any sense of superiority. The word restore that is used here is the same word that first century people used in medical language for the process of a broken bone being healed.

When I was sixteen years old, I broke my left arm in a trampoline accident. Three things immediately happened in my life.

I was taken to a hospital full of caring doctors and nurses. My arm was immobilized and wrapped in a thick cast. I did not participate in an sports or activity until the bone had fully healed.

Being in the hospital wasn't punitive. It was there to save me.

The immobilization wasn't punitive. It was for my own protection. Stepping away from what I love to do wasn't punitive. It was to insure that I could engage in sports again safely.

One of my life-long friends and now the Pastor at Church on the Move, Whit George, shared something with me a while back that I found insightful. One the reasons that God calls us into a tight-knit group of friends is because most of us are not self-aware enough to see the areas that need attention in our lives. We tend to accentuate all the good we see in ourselves and avoid our unbecoming traits or attitudes.

Vulnerable, transparent, restorative community is not an option if we are going to experience real resurrection.

Perhaps you've heard of this rat experiment from the 80's—you know, the one that became a pop ad for the Partnership for a Drug-Free America. It went like this. They had a rat in a cage, all by itself, with two water bottles. One bottle was water. The second bottle was water laced with cocaine. In the ad, it shows the rat continually scurrying to the drugged water, going back for more and more, until it is finally shown lying dead in the cage.

The advertisement spells it out:

"Only one drug is so addictive, nine out of ten laboratory rats will use it. And use it. And use it. Until dead. It's called cocaine. And it can do the same thing to you."

But there was a Canadian professor named Bruce Alexander who felt there was something messed up about this experiment. Why was the rat put in a cage alone? What else could it do but take the drugs? He wondered what would happen if it's environment was changed.

So Professor Alexander built an amazing Rat Park. It was paradise for rats. They had colored balls, great rat-food, and cool tunnels to scamper up and down. Most importantly, they had plenty of friends. Everything a rat about town could want. What happened? In the Rat Park, all the rats still tried both water bottles. But check this out. The "Rat Park" community of rodents didn't go for the drugged water. They almost totally shunned it and not one of them died.

If I was going to break out of my life-time of porn and sexual addiction, I had to get out of my cage that was both triggering and reinforcing my habitual behavior and embrace a new community that fostered deep and healthy relationships.

We cannot rise alone. I tried a thousand prayers alone.

I repented a thousand times alone. I cried a thousand tears alone. There are good people who will love you well. Who are they? Invite them in. Allow them to help you see the grave clothes that need to be removed. They are not befitting of who you really are. Let them go.

A robe of righteousness waits in your King's hands.
Made for you.

Chapter Twenty Eight

THERE ARE ALWAYS SNIPERS AT A RESURRECTION PARADE

"Real miracles bother people, like strange sudden pains unknown in medical literature. It's true: They rebut every rule all we good citizens take comfort in. Lazarus obeying orders and climbing up out of the grave - now there's a miracle, and you can bet it upset a lot of folks who were standing around at the time. When a person dies, the earth is generally unwilling to cough him back up. A miracle contradicts the will of the earth."

Leif Enger - American Author

Are you ready for this? When I read this postscript to the story of Lazarus, I nearly fell to the floor. John, one of Jesus' followers, pens these words in his gospel account …

"The large crowd of Jews discovered that he was there and came to the scene—not only because of Jesus but to catch sight of Lazarus, the man whom he had raised from the dead. Then the chief priests planned to kill Lazarus as well, because he was the reason for many of the Jews' going away and putting their faith in Jesus."

John 12: 9-11 J.B. Phillips Translation

Did you catch that? The religious henchmen were coming for Lazarus. Are you kidding me??? Lazarus has already died once, and they were coming to kill him again!

One of the truths I had to come to grips with in my resurrection journey is this: the miracle of resurrection in my life didn't always produce a line of cheerleaders. In fact, it created some enemies. What kind of enemies? I have identified two.

First, there are people. I began to realize there were folks that liked me better before. The clean, pristine Blaine. The hero that could do no wrong.

I remember teaching a message to church leaders years ago, "Why Disney World is the Happiest Place on Earth and the Church Isn't." I made a case that when people walk into our churches that they should feel like they are at Disney. You know … happy music, happy people, happy surroundings … HAPPY, HAPPY, HAPPY!

Actually no.

Disney isn't real. It is a staged production from the moment you walk in until the minute you leave. Mickey and Minnie Mouse have plastic, pre-formed smiles that never change. Allow me to take you to the real Disney. It's called Disney underground. It is a known fact that Disney World has a complexed matrix of tunnels and space below the Magic Kingdom where characters and employees prepare for their shifts, receive medical attention for dehydration and other health issues, or simply take breaks from being "on" all the time, catering to the demands of Disney guests.

Disney underground is the real Disney. The sweaty masks are taken off. Mishaps are managed. Injuries are cared for.

My new message to church leaders would be this. The church that Jesus called for ought to be much more like underground Disney than Disney World. Honest. Vulnerable. Masks off.

For way too many years, my life was a Hollywood movie town.

A wonderful collection of facades with nothing but emptiness behind the carefully maintained exterior. As consequential as it was, the best choice I ever made was to finally take my mask off. For better or worse, I got honest about following Jesus without posturing and pretense.

But there will be snipers when you get honest about resurrection and people will be quick to point out the dirt and the rags as you come up from your grave. And I get it. I betrayed the trust of family, friends, colleagues and thousands more who followed me from a distance. There was hurt and disgust when people learned about my hypocrisy.

There was a couple that attended our church in Frisco that I had helped and counseled dozens of times over the years we pastored there. We had become very close friends. She had admitted to lusting after other men in the church and he was continually falling into pornography, as well as battling clinical depression and suicide. I had spent countless hours in their home, praying for them and helping them to save their marriage. I'm not entirely sure how I was I able to do that, given my own sinful situation.

I guess I had this insane ability to compartmentalize. It was like I could divorce myself from my secret life and be a pastor when others needed me most. I was like King Saul when David took up his lyre and played. The evil spirits would leave and God's presence would come. And in those moments, it was real. I was real.

I truly did care and desperately wanted to see the lives of others transformed, even if my life was beyond repair.

Finishing the story, when my sin came out publicly, the husband asked to meet with me. Trying to hide my tears as we sat in a corner booth at International House of Pancakes in Frisco, I asked him to forgive me for my sins and told him how much we needed

151

their love and friendship right now.

I never heard from him again.

The sound of sniper shots were continually ringing out in my direction. All the scandalous whispers would eventually get back to me. One of the most beautiful friends God brought into my life is Ruth Graham. You may have heard of her dad, Dr. Billy Graham, perhaps the most significant evangelist in modern history. Ruth has an inspiring story of resurrection from betrayal, loss and pain in her life. I met her for the first time at a ministers roundtable in San Antonio. I remember writing down this little jewel in my iPhone as she shared that day …

"Jesus broke principles with people. We break people with principles."

So what did I do with the snipers in my life?

At first, I was embittered. The old adage would come up in my head, "The church is the only army that shoots it's wounded in battle." But over time, the Lord wooed me into compassion and understanding. There is an upshot to our sin. In many cases, it is devastating to those closest to us. Let them vent. Allow them to separate if they have to. It is not our job to control the response others have to our misdeeds. They have every right to feel the emotions they feel. And we must give people permission to grieve and respond in whatever way they are compelled to.

I had to learn to own my sin. Not play the blame game. Not return fire. Just keep walking away from the grave into His gloriously new resurrected life.

The second sniper is within. Our own thoughts and attitudes. You've heard the saying, "shoot yourself in the foot?" Well, there are times we shoot ourselves in the heart. Our internal snipers have names.

Shame.
Unforgiveness. Anger.
Hate.
The shots were going off in my head non-stop.
"You will never be happy again."
"You are worthless."
"No one will ever respect you."
"You think you are over this, but you will fail again."

The truth is, these snipers are more lethal than people. Because I could avoid people, but enemies like shame and anger went everywhere I went. Until I took them out. Not only did these hit-men make my existence miserably depressing, they also triggered relapses back into my addictive behavior. They had to go. But it wasn't easy.

One of the most brutal snipers in my life was the deadly force of unforgiveness. There were two people taking up malicious space in my head. Pastor Robert Morris and my former pastor, Willie George.

As I shared earlier, I was angry at the way Pastor Morris had responded to our family when Gateway Church assumed stewardship of our church campus following my resignation. I had gratitude that our church community was being shepherded, but I allowed resentment to build in my heart because of my own perceived lack of care for our family during this time.

I guess I looked at the thousands of dollars Gateway poured out to keep our church building afloat, while Cathy and I were financially drowning. The interminable buzz of bitterness in my head would not stop. The letter I had written him was filled with threats and scorn.

Several years later, I knew I had to make amends. It was eating me alive. I sent an email to his assistant pastor requesting the opportunity to meet with him. Pastor Morris quickly agreed and invited me to join him for lunch at his brand new church facility in Southlake, a sprawling suburb north of Dallas. I was apprehensive, to say the least. This was one of the most influential pastors in the nation and his church was quickly becoming one of the largest in the country. And I was the disgraced and prodigal pastor.

As I was escorted into a private room, Pastor Morris put his hand out and as I reached to shake it, he pulled me in and gave me a warm hug and greeting. Before I could apologize for my terrible letter, he asked me to forgive him for not being more attentive to our family during my transition out of Northstar Church. He treated me like a peer, without any air of superiority. He recieved my request for forgiveness and I parted that day with peace.

Then there was the broken relationship with my former pastor and mentor, Willie George. This was much more complicated because it involved my two oldest sons.

After moving to Dallas, Jeremy was starting to ask questions about his Christian faith. While he was very supportive of our new church plant and helped us with our video production every week, he was exploring a new world outside the Christian bubble he grew up in. He was trying to figure out what he believed about Jesus (or didn't believe) for himself. Word got back to some of his friends at Church on the Move in Tulsa that Jeremy was now an atheist—and that he was drinking and smoking … among other rumors I'm sure. Some of those closest to him, shut down their friendship with him.

On July 22, 2007 at 11:46pm, I received a text from one of Jeremy's friends in Tulsa. He had just spoken with Jeremy and feared he was about to take his life. Cathy and I frantically tried to call him—with no answer. We called again and again and again. Still f*cking nothing!! He had just moved to a new apartment downtown and we had no idea where it was. I was screaming at the phone … "Answer god-dammit!! Answer the phone!!!" Cathy was sobbing uncontrollably.

Finally—someone answered, "Hello?" I quickly retorted, "Is that you, Bub?" The voice on the other end said, "No sir, this is a paramedic. Who is calling?" I told him, "I'm Jeremy's father—is my son ok?" His response took the breath out of me, "I'm sorry sir, your son is unconscious. We are transporting him to Baylor Medical Center." I dropped the phone, grabbed Cathy and we sped down the expressway to the hospital.

When we arrived, doctors told us that he downed a bottle of Advil and chased it with several bottles of beer. It was written up as a suicide attempt. He was still unconscious. They administered something called hemoperfusion, which is a technique used to treat a drug overdose, where the patient's blood is filtered through some kind of charcoal. An hour or so later, a doctor approached us in the waiting room, "You son has regained consciousness." Tears of joy rushed from our eyes. We ran into his hospital room and just hugged him. We couldn't stop and didn't want to let him go. Our son was alive.

A day later, we drove him home. Cathy and I were in emotional ruins. We just held each other and sobbed.

How close had we come to losing our boy?
How deep had his pain been that he would rather die than live?
How could we be so blind to our son's grappling with life?

When we felt like Jeremy was emotionally capable of talking about what happened, we asked the question that had been hanging in the air for more than a week. He knew before I could get out of my mouth what it was. Why Bub? He was immersed in remorse for what he had done. Though he refused to blame a soul for his actions, he described the awful pain he felt from the rejection of his Christian friends in Tulsa. He was just in a place of deep loneliness and isolation.

We were absolutely heart-broken. And at least for me, bitterness began to set in toward Pastor George and Church on the

Move. What the hell kind of Christianity was this? One of their spiritual sons goes astray and they slam the gate to Father's house? Somehow it got back to me that Jeremy was being talk- ed about disparagingly in a senior department head meetings at Church on the Move along with the judgement that was going to come to his doorstep. Whether this was true or not, I believed it and was angry.

Then a few months after his attempted suicide, Jeremy got into a text war with one of his former best friends, who was employed at Church on the Move. Admittedly, he used the Lord's name in vain along with a spell of other profanity toward this friend and the church. Within a day, the texts had been shared with Pastor George and he was on the phone to me.

"Blaine, I need you and Cathy to come and meet with me in Tulsa," he said somberly. "I think you have some serious problems with your boys and we want to get it worked out with you." He went on to say he was rescinding several invitations I had been given to speak at Church on the Move. My immediate feelings were … why was I being punished and held accountable for the actions of my adult children? None of our children were living in our home. The lives they were choosing to live was beyond my scope of control. Plus, I reflected on the times that I had walked Pastor George's own kids through their own struggles. Did he think his kids were all perfect? The more I thought about it, the angrier I got.

I hastily overnighted him a letter telling him he was wrong and that we would not meet with him under the circumstances he was demanding of us. A few days later, I received a letter back with Pastor George's resignation from our board of Trustees.

I did not speak with him again for six years.

What I did not tell Cathy and my sons at the time was this: though I was unquestionable upset at the way Jeremy had been treated, there was a deeper reason for my resistance toward Pastor

George prying into our lives. I was gripped with an underlying fear that the dirt of my secret life might be unearthed if I let him get too close.

The lies. The failure. The death.

I reasoned that I couldn't risk Cathy breaking down and disclosing the sham that our marriage had become? Or what if Willie asked me if there was any hidden sin in my own life—all I knew was I wanted no part of a meeting.

Today, I regret the way I responded to my Pastor. I was wrong. I was hiding. I should have just manned up and met with him— worked out the differences and confessed to my own sinful secrets. I do believe today that had I agreed to meet with him, he would have worked to help us the best he knew how. But my sorrow extends on an even greater level to my boys. I wasn't honest with them. I feel like I used them as pawns to avoid any accountability for the terrible secrets in my own life. And God only knows how much my sin created gaps in my ability to be a present and faithful father to them.

We don't get do-overs in life, but if we did, I would give anything to do fatherhood better.

In the years following my confession, I sent a letter asking to meet with Pastor George to personally seek forgiveness for my sin. His return letter was polite but clear. He was not interested in meeting with me at this time, indicating a need for the fruits of repentance to be completely evident in my life. While I didn't understand his rejection at the time, I do now. I had spoken with ill-will towards him in both private and public settings and I know my words got back to him. Putting myself in his shoes, I can only surmise what his thoughts might have been … perhaps something like this …

"I gave Blaine so many opportunities … *Fire by Nite* …

Oneighty … and then helped him raise up a team—along with a gift of several hundred thousand dollars to plant his own church in Dallas. And the moment I ask him for a simple meeting, he bails on me. And then I find out that he has been perpetrating this elaborate double life the entire time."

Regardless of what his exact thoughts towards me were, I know now he had a reason to feel betrayed. Receiving his letter rejecting my earnest plea for forgiveness and reconciliation was heart-rending. He had been like a spiritual father. At the end of the day, I still had appreciation and love for him. And I was grateful for the things he had done for me. I just longed for things to be right with us.

I didn't give up. I kept my heart in tact. And I sent him another letter in the spring of 2015. He agreed to meet. I remember walking up to the Starbucks in Utica Square, a quaint outdoor shopping area in the heart of Tulsa. There he was—sitting at an outdoor table. Any unease I had in that moment was dispelled when he rose from his chair with a gentle smile and hugging me said, "It's good to see you again Blaine." I asked him for his forgiveness and he granted absolution.

As we parted that day, the sun broke through the morning clouds. I just looked up and let the warmth of it's glow touch my face. It was as if God was smiling. All the bitterness and pain of the past washed away like dead leaves overcome by a mountain stream.

I was free.

Don't let the snipers ruin your resurrection parade. Remove them from their poisonous perch. Run to the Father. Let him work with the angry big brothers and your shame-filled past.

He has rings and robes. Music and cheer. Feasts and forgiveness.

Welcome home.

Chapter Twenty Nine

RESURRECTED PEOPLE TAKE
LONG WALKS IN CEMETERIES

It was another morning.

I woke up at around 7:00am, as the sun rose, breaking through the bedroom window of my downtown Dallas apartment. The only way to describe the first two years of my attempt to recover some semblance of life was—punishing. Not only was I slogging away in my bid for freedom from sin and addiction, but I was also encountering a savage new enemy.

Depression.

And this word does not even do it justice. I'm not talking about sadness. I had been sad before. How could I possibly describe what was going on in my soul?

Imagine the worst day of your life.

You lost your mother or father to a tragic death.
Your son or daughter was diagnosed with a horrific disease.
You landed in prison for a crime you didn't commit.
You woke up to discover your wife had left you.
Remember how the darkness felt in the worst part of that day?

Now imagine never being able to escape that darkness. Feeling the entire world collapsing on you every hour, every day—without consolation. The only thing I wanted to do was sleep. Because it was the only reasonable way to escape.

Well intentioned friends and family would try to root out the source of my despondency. Exasperated, I would think to myself, "I have no f*cking idea why I feel like killing myself ... every single moment ... of every single day ... but that's the damned reality." Instead, I would simply lift my eyes and try to assuage their con- cerns, "I really have no idea why I can't get past this. I really want to be happy again ... I just can't right now."

One of my counselors told me that it takes an entire year of grieving following one catastrophic personal event. Things like the loss of a marriage. End of a career. Financial ruin. Public humiliation. I had experienced all of these. In one horrific year. The grief was unbearable.

As I rolled out of my bed, my head was going in a thousand directions. I had been working for a non-profit organization based out of Dallas, called Bully Proof USA. We were putting on public school assemblies in an effort to curb the bullying problem in America. I was the marketing director and while it was a great job, our corporate funding had run out and I had just been informed by our board of directors that we were shutting things down.

What now?

As I sank into my favorite leather chair with my morning coffee, I opened my computer to read the morning news and check my email. A Facebook message notification popped up in the corner of my laptop. It was from Pastor Gregory Dickow. Huh?? I had seen Pastor Dickow on Christian television, (and always thought he was one of the good guys) but I had never met him. I opened his message ...

"Hey Blaine, I hope you're doing well. I'm looking for someone who can link arms with me to change the world. The position is: Strategic Global Growth Director."

Within hours we were on the phone together. He explained that the Lord had awakened him at 4:15 that morning and he couldn't go back to sleep. He felt prompted to invite me to join his staff team. I asked, "Pastor, do you have any idea what happened in my life two years ago?" He told me no. I shared my story with him and he said these exact words, "I believe in God's healing and restoration in your life. The route you took to get where you are today sure wasn't the one you would have ever hoped or wished for; but even in your darkest and lowest season, God graciously and lovingly has kept you; and is turning the darkness into light. You might as well start packing your suitcases."

As I hung up the phone, my eyes began to water up—how could God be so good to me? For the first time in a long, long time, I felt his presence and favor in my life. A quiet hope began to surface in my soul.

Thirty days later, I was sitting in my new office at Life Changers International Church in a suburb of Chicago, looking out my window at the beautiful pond behind the church, filled with Canadian geese. How fitting … one Canadian goose looking out at a flock of others. My first day on my new job was November 1st—my birthday. That moment wasn't lost on me as I surveyed this beau- tiful gift of God's grace.

I was bringing my talents to bear once again in His Church. I had a Pastor and church family who believed in me.

Over the coming year, as I served the vision of Pastor Dickow, little by little, the Lord began to impart a longing into my heart to help others who have been overcome by pornography and sexual brokenness. Somehow, I believed that God wasn't going to allow my past to go to waste. As I shared this with Pastor Dickow one spring afternoon in his office, he reached out with a firm grip on my forearm and spoke these words into my heart, "Blaine, your calling is always in your conquering."

BOOM!!

My thoughts went back to the story of Lazarus. According to Eastern Orthodox Church tradition, sometime after the resurrection of Christ, Lazarus was forced to flee Judea because of rumored plots on his life. So he moved to Cyprus. There he was appointed by Paul and Barnabas as the first Bishop of Kition (present-day Larnaka). He lived there for thirty more years, shepherding his church with love and care until his death eighteen years later.

Can you imagine "Brother Levi" coming in for a counseling appointment with Pastor Lazarus?

Brother Levi: Pastor, I feel like I've come to a dead-end in my life.

Pastor Lazarus: Well, nothing is too hard for Jesus my dear one.

Brother Levi: No you don't understand. I feel like death is all around me.

Pastor Lazarus: Uh … yes sir. Actually, I do understand.

Brother Levi: Well … I doubt you have ever felt completely hopeless like me.

Pastor Lazarus: Well. I died once. Was in a grave for four days. Definitely despondent at the time.

Brother Levi: Ok then.

God spoke to a young man named Jeremiah who, like me, had

a propensity for questioning his ability and qualifications …

> "I knew you before I formed you in your mother's womb.
> Before you were born I set you apart and appointed you
> as my prophet to the nations."

Jeremiah 1:5 New Living Translation

I don't believe God wants us to discover our work calling—but rather our womb calling. Mark Twain has been credited with this profound thought … "There are two great days in a person's life—the day we are born and the day we discover why." I believe those who genuinely experience the grace of a Jesus' resurrection in their life, love to take long walks in cemeteries. That is … there is this deep sense that God is going to use our coming forth from death to rescue others who are still trapped in their graves of sin and brokenness. Resurrection people have a keen sense for the smell of death. We sniff it out and are always trusting Jesus to call life into the lifeless.

My next stop in my resurrection journey would be back to my old stomping grounds in Tulsa, Oklahoma. In hindsight, I can see how the Lord orchestrated each step I was taking out of my grave and into a new life that was previously unimaginable. Pastors, friends, colleagues, counselors and co-workers were pouring hope and freedom into my soul. Knowing I was supposed to be back in Tulsa and close to my family and so many friends I grew up with, I called Ron Luce to catch him up on my plans. He quickly encouraged me, "Blaine, you need to check out Pastors Ed Gungor and Brent Sharpe, who co-pastor Sanctuary Church." So I did.

I walked into Sanctuary for the first time, and within moments people were welcoming me—some who knew me or others who didn't know me from a bar of soap. Pastor Ed quickly found me and ushered me up to the front row to sit with him during worship before he would get up to preach. The best way to describe the service that Saturday evening was a cool amalgamation of

Pentecostals, Catholics and Jesus. It was life-giving and liturgical all at the same time. Living mostly in a pentecostal world most of my life, I had come to stereotype any forms of liturgy as stale, traditional and dead.

But this surprised me. As we declared the Apostle's Creed together, I felt the strength of our belief as a community. Being invited to participate and see Jesus in the Lord's Table each week had a profound effect in my learning to walk faithfully. We prayed community prayers, put ash crosses on foreheads, observed Lent and followed the liturgical calendar. There was a distinct emphasis on the early church fathers and I loved all that I was learning about the first century church.

I felt like Sanctuary took me back to the roots of my Christian faith. Before the hype and the marketing. Before it was popular to be a Christian. When martyrdom was common and following Jesus was more about breaking bread than not breaking the rules. I fell in love with this community.

A few months later, Ed and Brent invited me to join the staff team as the Operations Pastor, helping to oversee the various ministries of the church.

Ed had been through a painful personal crisis seventeen years earlier and he and his wonderful wife, Gail, had rebuilt their lives and family together. They opened their hearts to me and their story gave me hope. Brent and his wife Janis were licensed family counselors and every Thursday morning, Brent and I would meet and he would spill strength into my soul. These would be years of intensive healing and where I would finally experience total freedom from the heavy chains of my addiction.

But there was something else. They invited me to preach again in the church. They actually were trusting me once again to stand before God's people and speak the Word of the Lord. It had been three years since I had brought a pastoral sermon to a congregation. I prayed earnestly over my message that Sunday and shared a sermon titled, "Where Prodigals Party—Being the Community God Dreamed of."

When the service ended, there was a stream of people shaking my hand and hugging my neck, telling me how much my words had impacted their life that morning. Some were visibly touched, tears streaming down their eyes. One older gentleman waited until everyone else had left the auditorium. He finally approached me, "Pastor Blaine, I had given up hope for my life. It's not that I thought my sin was too great for God to forgive. It was just that I didn't believe I could actually stop. This morning, the Lord used you to give me the promise of true freedom."

Wow. I was a pastor again. And somehow, the Lord was present in whatever awkward way His word came out of my mouth that day. And at least one man needed to hear my story.

When we unearth our reason for resurrection and dare to believe it—all of heaven conspires to bring it to pass.

There was however one last part of my life that remained empty. That was about to change.

Chapter Thirty

RESURRECTIONS COST
MORE THAN FUNERALS

When God looked down at Adam, he took a thorough assessment of his situation and concluded, "It is not good for man to be alone."

In the four years following my divorce, one of the most perplexing undertakings was learning to live single. On one hand, there was a certain amount of freedom to living alone. I could make my own schedule. Come and go at my leisure. Basically be center of my universe. But this new-found independence was far outweighed by outright loneliness. I missed having a partner in life. You can only play so many hands of solitaire on a Saturday night.

I eased back into the dating world rather slowly. For a couple reasons. First, I was still getting my training wheels under me in my recovery. I was re-learning real love. When you have objectified women for as long as I did in my secret world, there was a need for radical change in my headspace. Women, as a sex addict, were always a means to an end for me. I would dehumanize and disregard the fact that every woman is an image-bearer of our Creator, a beloved daughter to our Heavenly Father.

Secondly, I honestly just didn't want to boomerang out of my divorce into a hasty relationship that would become a set up for yet another failure in my life. And God was working deeply in me on this thing called surrender.

I believe the prospect of truly embracing resurrection in our life is an expensive one. The plain truth is, resurrections cost more than funerals. Not many days after Jesus called forth life into Lazarus's cold dead frame, Lazarus hosted a "Let's Thank Jesus" dinner party. Which was totally appropriate. When a friend shows up at your funeral and decides to give you a second shot at life, thanks are in order.

Here's how it went down.

"Six days before Passover, Jesus entered Bethany where Lazarus, so recently raised from the dead, was living. Lazarus and his sisters invited Jesus to dinner at their home. Martha served. Lazarus was one of those sitting at the table with them. Mary came in with a jar of very expensive aromatic oils, anointed and massaged Jesus' feet, and then wiped them with her hair. The fragrance of the oils filled the house."

John 12:1-5 The Message Translation

Big parties cost money. Food, drink, decorations … and then there was the jar of oil used to anoint Jesus' feet. Anointing someone's head or body was a common practice with the Jews. It was a sign of respect and deep gratitude. And when someone had saved your life from harm or certain death, it was customary to kiss and anoint the feet of the one who saved you.

The cost of the aromatic oil used that night translates to about $50,000 of our dollars. It was so pricey that Judas, Jesus' treasurer, about blew a gasket at the perceived waste. As the man of the house, I can guarantee you that Lazarus stepped up to the plate on the bill for this entire evening of celebration.

As I began to experience this new capacity for resurrection in my life, it was accompanied by a bottomless gratitude of the heart. This new Jesus life could only be lived with a dangerous and expensive loyalty. Without surrender, it was just a return to another unremarkable, unexceptional, garden-variety version of Christianity. And I wasn't interested in that. So I had inaugurated a new kind of devotion in my life.

Today, one of my daily rituals is to pray The Lord's Prayer. According to *The Didache*, a first century Christian practice manual compiled by the Apostles, it was the custom of early believers to pray The Lord's Prayer three times each day. I love each part of this prayer that Jesus taught us to pray, but this piece sends me back to my knees each morning ...

"Thy will be done on earth as it is in heaven."

For me, each day is about inviting all the intentions of heaven to trump the messiness of my earthly efforts to live. I had always been good at controlling and manipulating a situation, and sadly, people as well. I demanded control. Not having it, scared the hell out of me. I wanted to have relationships on my terms, not yours.

And I sure as shootin' wasn't letting God have the final say in any part of my life. While he may have started as Lord of my life, I had bargained him down to more of silent partner in the business of making ministry happen.

So here I was, recklessly inviting this spirit of surrender into new parts of my life.

My sexuality.
My money.
My work.
And my singleness.

As I began to figure out how to legitimately meet a woman that

169

had the same kind of desire for God that I did, I struggled. I am somewhat of an introvert, so I'm not the guy that is going to walk up to a woman in a grocery store and ask her what aisle the Corn Flakes are on, followed by, "Whacha up to Friday night, my little Walmart wonder?" And finding a date while attending a church just felt kind of weird for me. I felt reluctant to scan the auditorium as I entered to try to find someone attractive to worship beside. And it's kind of awkward walking out of a service, to tap a woman on the shoulder and say, "Hey, I know I'm a total stranger, but your hair is like a flock of goats. Wanna study *The Purpose Driven Life* together?"

So I joined an online dating site. And oh ... the stories.

You're always taking a chance dating someone you've never met. You just have to be prepared for the worst possible outcome. Profile pictures were often ten (or twenty) years younger than a person's actual age. One night I walked into a restaurant and a lady who looked like she was in her seventies walked up to me and said, "You must be Blaine!" And I said, "And you must be Grandma." I didn't say that. Because I'm kinder than that. But I thought it.

I remember another date all too well. To my astonishment, this lady was as attractive as her picture and as we sat down for dinner, our conversation was warm and I could tell a connection was building. Our values and faith were in sync. Finally, I thought ... this is going to be the beginning of something really wonderful.

And then the question—"So Blaine, what happened in your first marriage?" Sheesh ... uh ... how about I was a schmuck-struttin-turd-burglar? But ... rather than control and manipulate my desired outcome with this date, I settled on the truth. Complete honesty.

When I finished, she politely looked across our half-eaten steak dinners and went into counselor mode, "Blaine, I might advise you on future dates, that will not include me, to restrain yourself from being so honest." And with that, our dated ended. As I walked out and said goodbye, it was impossible to hide my sadness. Sometimes life really hurts. My past was forgiven. But how long would it continue to sabotage me?

Yet as testing as it was, I continued to embrace surrender. Live each day with Jesus. Walk honestly. Serve humbly. Let him be Lord of the outcome.

And then it happened. Seated in the waiting area of Ti Amo's in Tulsa, a quaint little Italian restaurant, in walked a woman I can only describe as pure elegance. She was breathtaking. I asked if she was Lori, and to my delight, she smiled and said "I am ... are you Blaine?" And the night took off—until I asked her this question, "What are you looking for in a man?" Laying her fork down, a solemn look came across her countenance, "I'm pretty open— but I can't handle someone coming out of addiction."

Strike one, two and three. All in one answer.

But to my utter surprise, as I shared parts of my story with Lori that evening, she didn't hit eject. She told me later that my cologne and my shoes got me a second date. I'm not sure what got me our third date, but there was some kind of mystery unfolding between us. Lori was a dental hygienist who had grown up in the Methodist Church and had a beautiful daughter, Ally, who was attending college. Lori had tried valiantly to hold on to her first marriage, but after seventeen years, her ex-husband's struggle with alcohol became untenable. (thus her aversion to addiction issues)

Lori was working through her own surrender issues. A month before we met, she had come home after a somewhat disastrous date, and told God, "I give up. Unless you bring me a godly man, I am done with the dating world." One of the things that attracted me to Lori was her complete lack of desire to control the outcome of our relationship. We were having fun. Riding my motorcycle. Going to movies. Trying new restaurants. And going to see

"Hook," our favorite Tulsa band. I never felt any pressure from Lori. The truth is, she didn't need a guy. She was secure in herself, made a good living, had good friends, a wonderful family and enjoyed her independence.

I remember having dinner together about five months into our relationship. Still somewhat in dating mode, we weren't really "a couple" yet. Almost out of the blue, she said, "If you really want me, you're going to have to get serious about chasing me down." I thought, this is my kind of girl. She respects herself. She has confidence. And she isn't about to settle for anything less than God's prize for her life. And at that moment—I was determined to be her prize.

I dropped off care packages at her door when she was sick. I washed her car. Paid for every date. I kept all the flower shops in business around my house. I was falling head over heels in love with her. As I thought about proposing to her, I went down her long list of qualities and then tried to find some kind of chink in her armor ... surely she wasn't perfect? What was I missing? I was getting so close to asking for her hand in marriage. And then the tipping point came.

We were having dinner on an outdoor patio at Full Moon Cafe on Cherry Street, near downtown Tulsa. As I nursed a post-dinner glass of merlot, I put my hand on Lori's. "Babe, I just going to lay it all out there. For better or worse, this is me." Somewhere between anticipation and bewilderment, she replied, "Please tell me what's on you heart, Blaine." My next words were right to the point, "You know my past. And I don't make a lot of money. I live in a one room apartment. But I believe in the God who makes Picassos out of finger paintings. And I love you. And whatever God has for my life will be a millions times better with you."

She looked back at me as I patiently waited for her response ... "I love you too Blaine. And I don't care if we live in a trailer the rest of our lives, I am so proud of the man that you are today. And

I want to be on your arm." My eyes were betrayed by my tears, as a lengthy smile broke across my face ... and trying to sniff discretely, I pulled my angel from heaven close and never let her go again.

The love that I felt that night from that girl changed everything. I had just experienced a piece of heaven. She knew everything about me and still loved me. She saw a surrendered man. A resurrected man. And I was looking across at a woman that was the perfect picture of grace.

We married the following spring. My boys and my family love Lori and I feel the same love for Ally and the rest of Lori's family. Now in our fifth year of marriage, we're happier than a sackful of puppies. Lori is a dream come true. She is smarter than me. Better looking than me. But I'm better at hockey. We are inseparable—do everything together, from grocery shopping to our nightly talks on the porch.

And together, we remain surrendered to him. We've lost our lives in Jesus. Clinging to his words ...

"Whoever does not take up their cross and follow me is not worthy of me. Whoever finds their life will lose it, and whoever loses their life for my sake will find it"

Matthew 10:38-39 New International Version

Everyone wants a resurrection, but no one wants to die. We experience resurrection when we are willing to confront the parts of our life that must be brought to death.

Sin.
Ego.
Certainty.
Look at me.
The need to be right.

My list can be endless at times. But I've learned how to die. That each time I find "self" efforting to push it's way to the front of the line … I must find my way back to the cross.

Let go.

Stop managing your reputation. Quit hiding behind someone that isn't really you. Refuse to give into the notion that the stuff you covet will actu- ally satisfy.

Find your cross. Pick it up. Because the minute we give it all up—lose everything.

Life finds us.

EPILOGUE

First things first.

Please forgive me. Maybe we've met. Perhaps not. But I know the impact of my sin was felt far beyond my own family and friends and one reason I wrote this book is to publicly ask forgiveness for my sin. So many felt lied to—and betrayed. I just want you to know how deep my sorrow is for my past life.

Secondly, I didn't write this book to blow sunshine up your posterior.

On-earth resurrections, while glorious in their transformation of the human soul, are still a human endeavor. They take place in damaged people with earth-suits like you and me. We still wake up each morning to the news of murdering psychopaths, meth addicted mothers and fathers, starving children, hating racists, and a thousand other blights on our human existence.

But we also wake up to us. To our mortal struggle.

What I am about to tell you is conveyed with the utmost gratitude and humility. I am in my seventh year of complete freedom from pornography and acting out sexually. Not one relapse. And in sharing this, I can only do so while expressing profound gratitude to Jesus and every single person who has invested in my resurrection.

People who attend my speaking engagements or read my blogs or social media posts, repeatedly ask me this question, "Blaine, what is the one thing more than anything else that has been the secret to your resurrection out of sexual addiction?" Unequivocally, my reply is always as follows, "Embracing the pain while exposing the lies."

I had to let go of every lie that held me hostage. And choose to believe a new treasury of truths that would set me free.

Truths like these: I can trust those who love me most with my secrets. Sharing my truth doesn't get me in trouble. It gets me out of trouble. The church isn't a gallery for the good, but a hospital for the hopeless. I can't earn the love of the Savior. The account's already settled. And I'm in the plus column. The loved forever column—the never let you go column.

And my past does not define me.

I am Blaine Bartel.
I am Jonah after the whale.
I am Peter after Pentecost.
I am Paul after a dirty Damascus road.
I am a resurrection man.

I remember sitting in an addiction recovery group as men introduced themselves around the circle. ""I'm Joe and I'm an alcoholic." "I'm Doug and I'm a sex addict." You get the gist. I was next. "I'm Blaine and I am a child of God who is learning to overcome sex addiction." There was a hush that came over the group. I had broken the code. Own who you are. But I am not my behavior. And I am not my past. We will never rise higher than who we believe we really are.

Yet I have also pledged to remember the pain. I will never forget the pain I caused Cathy, sobbing through the anguish of betrayal. I will never forget the pain I caused Jeremy, Dillon and Brock, and the gut-punch-realization that their father had become a fraud. And I will never forget the arrant look of sadness on the faces of my Mum and Dad, as their first-born went down in flames.

And with each sorrowful episode cached in my memory bank, I am constrained to never again allow my selfish un-doings to beget this kind of heartache in the people I love the most in this world.

And you need to know this. It took many failures along the way in the early stages of my inelegant stumbling out of the grave. The dirt and rags and stench didn't go away in one swell moment. I was in a death-match for my soul. There were more times than not that I pushed off the canvas, while the deafening demons in my head bellowed their ten count.

There were moments alone at the bottomless pit of depression, when I mulled, "What if Lazarus's resurrection was a stroke of bad luck? What if he hated his life and was glad it was finally over?" Because more days than not, that's where my madness took me in the early stages of my fight back.

"Is this really worth whatever sliver of strength I have left?"
"What if freedom is a fabricated freaking fairy tale?"
"And where the hell is God today?"

Each time these desperate questions would come … if I would wait long enough … and turn my heart just one more time to heaven … it was as if I could feel Jesus put his scarred hand to my ear … and hear His soothing whisper, "I'm listening. And I'm right here." I learned to be at peace with my desperation—Ok with the mystery of what tomorrow might bring. I stopped presuming Jesus was only around to multiply my loaves and fishes … and started to embrace His invitation to Gethsemane's garden.

To pray with him. To weep with him. To resist with him.

I will say it again. Resurrections are always late. What matters is you are undead. Dig out of the damn dirt and get to work on what you were born for.

Which begs the most perplexing question of being entrusted

with new breath in dead lungs, "What now?"

My bucket list was filled by the time I was forty. Money, celebrity, pleasure and achievement all seem rather meaningless today. I have experienced and accomplished more than I ever dreamed of, and it all fell spectacularly short of bagging even a backpack of the bliss my soul craved.

I have often found myself lingering in the shadows of Solomon's refrain …

"I have seen all the things that are done under the sun; all of them are meaningless, a chasing after the wind."

Ecclesiastes 1:14 New International Version

I love Jim Carrey. He is funny. And he is Canadian. I read an article recently about a kind of spiritual resurrection that Jim has experienced in his own life. One of the comments he made was striking, "I hope everyone could get rich and famous and have everything they ever dreamed of—so they will know it's not the answer."

How is the resurrected Blaine Bartel going to pursue life?

Should I make it my aim to travel the world again and speak to thousands about conquering their failures and addiction? Perhaps write my next best-selling book? Get out there and re-earn all the money I lost? Was I going to sign up all over again for my threadbare, moth-eaten, wind-chasing life? Same song, different chorus?

What could I possibly put in my bucket now? Something that would really count. The kind of stuff I would be proud to carry around and share with my family and friends?

I've been searching. Hard.
And a few nights ago, I found it.

It was Mum and Dad's sixtieth anniversary party. Think about that. Now both in their eighties, they have spent sixty years loving each other perfectly. At least that's what I thought.

After a meal together, our family and a few friends shared congratulations and tributes. My time came. My eyes glanced across the room, slowly landing on my Dad. Any notion of trying to prove myself to him had long since passed. He was my father. Not my competitor. I finally spoke up, "Dad, you have been the perfect father to me. I honestly can't think of a kinder, more unselfish man than you. I want to do business like you. I want to do friendship like you. I want to do family like you. And I want to do life like you."

My gaze then moved right to the very one who had brought me into this world, "Mum, You have been the Jesus compass in my life—through every adversity. Not just pointing me back to Jesus—but revealing Jesus in the beautiful way you live."

And then, out of the blue, my sister Luanne interjected a question, "Mum and Dad, what has been the secret to a lifetime of love and marriage?"

Silence.

It was as if Mum and Dad were contemplating the the implications of their answer. Finally Dad nervously laughed, "Well, there was a pretty good period of time when things weren't very good at all." Mum nodded in agreement, "We really didn't know if we were going to make it. We had come to a point where we felt divorce was our only option."

We all just sat there stunned. Did Mum just say divorce? I couldn't even remember my Mum and Dad having a good old fashioned blowup, never mind the talk of divorce. Breaking the speechlessness of the moment, I sputtered, "Whoa, whoa … did you say you were mulling over divorce?? When the heck was this?" Everyone in the room leaned forward as if we were all about to unearth the payoff in a mystery movie.

Mum shared in the most honest moment I had ever seen between the two of them, "Well, Dad was working way too much … gone all the time with the restaurants we owned. Sixteen hour days and weekends caused us to grow apart and it wasn't long before I was overwhelmed with fatigue and depression trying to raise our family alone …"

Trying to find the right words, Dad picked up the explanation, "Then … and the problem became … when I did get home, I was exhausted …" and looking almost mournfully at Mum, "… and your Mum would get angry with me … and I would just start looking for a reason to get back to work and out of the house."

Then Luanne asked the question we were all thinking. "What happened?"

Mum asserted, "Blaine." Huh?

She explained as she looked my way, "You just came home one night from church a very different kid. You were happy, carrying your Bible everywhere, and I finally told your Dad, 'You can do whatever you want, but I'm gathering up Jason and Luanne and taking them to Blaine's church tonight.'

Then she told us how she devoted her life to following Jesus that evening and a couple weeks later my Dad joined her and he relinquished his life to Christ as well. "In the months to come, God began healing our marriage and the Lord prompted your father to sell his businesses and begin a new career that would allow him to be the husband and father he wanted to be," Mum concluded.

As Lori and I drove home, I was bewildered. I knew my witness for Christ as a sixteen year old shaver on a quest for love and peace had a direct impact in Mum and Dad coming to Jesus. But had I been an unwitting instrument in the hands of God to actually save my own parents marriage? It appeared so.

And suddenly it became apparent that the greatest change I had ever been used to bring into this world was a quiet, private transformation that happened forty years ago—that I knew nothing about. And it had nothing to do with my efforts or well planned ministry strategies. I was just living. Resurrected.

Dear friends, I've made peace with the illusion that it was ever about changing the world. I'm just not as big a deal as I believed I was ... and yet every bit as big a deal as Jesus says I am. Figure that out.

Perhaps living a Jesus life means something more ... and even something less ... than seizing attention-grabbing headlines that justify my place in this world. Maybe the notion of becoming some kind of Christian phenom, was not only arrogant, but sadly misguided.

Could it be that leading a life, brimming with meaning and joy is not about changing the world—but allowing the beauty of God's messy humans to change us?

The beauty of Ron Luce, whose friendship is as sure as the morning sun.

The beauty of Dr. Ken McGill, who braved the loss of his own daughter to comfort me in my grief.

The beauty of a Mum and Dad, who trudged into my filthy grave and helped pull me out.

The beauty of Dillon, who looked past my double-dealing life, to impart a gift of love I could never earn.

The beauty of Cathy, who embodies the very essence of Jesus.

The beauty of Brock, who reminds me everyday that life is in the living.

The beauty of Jeremy, who had the courage to ask the dangerous questions.

The beauty of my bride Lori, who believes in the man I am, rather than the man I used to be.

The beauty of a thousand friends and family who said, "You are forgiven" and meant it.

And the beauty of Jesus who saves us all a seat at His table, with an amaranthine supply of bread and wine.

There's a story about a man who approached Mother Teresa and queried, "Mother, I want to do something great for God, but I don't know what. Should I start a school, be a missionary in a foreign land, build up a charitable agency?" He had great aspirations for God. Mother Teresa looked at him punctiliously and kindly responded: "What you need to do is make sure that no one in your family goes unloved."

You see, it was never about checking off a list to fill my bucket.

I believe the Psalmist got it right in his familiar prose, "You anoint my head with oil; my cup overflows." Maybe … just maybe … it's about receiving all the wonder of God's good grace in our lives, until our bucket spills over into the lives of those we bump into each day. That instead of buying bigger cups or bargaining God for a bigger bucket, we find significance in the spill.

Just know this. You matter. And the life you choose to live matters to those you love, in ways you'll never fully know.

Don't settle for a recovery when Jesus is handing out resurrections.

I think back to those stained glass windows in McKillop United Church that continually captured my gaze as a young boy.

Not long ago, I stumbled on to the origins of these magnificent mosaics. It turns out that a Catholic monk in the Middle Ages named Theophilus, gathered together hundreds of broken pieces of colored glass, attentively fused them together, one by one, fashioning a window for his abbey.

Tilted toward the sun, the imagery of this multi-colored masterpiece was unmistakeable—filtering a thousand colors of its Creator, touching the sun-warmed faces of his cobbled together community.

All we were ever meant to do was reflect the Son.

Broken.
Stained.
Somehow beauty.

ABOUT THE AUTHOR

Blaine is a Jesus guy. The Jesus he discovered in the ancient writings of canon. The one early church fathers were martyred for. The one who came for the poor, the broken and the captive. Because that's who Blaine was. Impoverished in soul. Broken in heart. Captive to lust and addiction. This Jesus yanked him out of the grave and graced him with Life 2.0. Blaine's accomplice in resurrection is his treasured wife Lori and he is the proud father of his beloved sons, Jeremy, Dillon and Brock.

Blaine is travels the world communicating both the story of Jesus and the account of his own resurrection from a self-inflicted death. Audiences find him beautifully raw, a compelling storyteller and unpredictably funny. He is an award-winning writer and the author of the best-selling *Little Black Book* series. Those who grew up in the 80's remember Blaine as the host of the popular faith-based television show *Fire by Nite*. During the 90's Blaine focused his attention on building the largest student outreach in America, attracting 2,500 teenagers weekly at Oneighty.

Today, Blaine professionally coaches men all over the world, guiding them out of unhealthy and unmanageable behavior into a life of authentic freedom and profound purpose. He is also a media creator and filmmaker, telling stories with short films and documentaries.

A Canadian raised in Calgary, Alberta, Blaine still plays hockey in a weekly beer league and has not yet given up his dream of joining the Royal Canadian Mounted Police. He and Lori enjoy grocery shopping together at Target, rattling on about life on a beach and watching their favorite Netflix series each night in bed.

CONTACT BLAINE

To contact Blaine for more information about his speaking, writing, coaching or filmmaking, please reach out through one of the following:

blainebartel.com

bbartel99@gmail.com

facebook.com/blainebartel777

twitter.com/blainebartel99

Made in the USA
Columbia, SC
09 June 2022

61494406R00111